ESSEN

JAGUAR XK
XK120/140/150

ESSENTIAL
JAGUAR XK
XK120/140/150

THE CARS AND THEIR STORY
1949-61

MIKE LAWRENCE

SPECIAL PHOTOGRAPHY BY
TONY BAKER AND JOHN COLLEY

BAY VIEW BOOKS

Published 1995 by Bay View Books Ltd
The Red House, 25-26 Bridgeland Street,
Bideford, Devon EX39 2PZ

© Copyright 1995 by Bay View Books Ltd
Edited by Mark Hughes
Typesetting and design by Chris Fayers & Sarah Ward

ISBN 1 870979 61 3
Printed in Hong Kong

CONTENTS

BIRTH OF THE XK

Launched in 1931, the rakish SS1, seen here in close-coupled coupé form (left), demonstrated William Lyons' belief that it cost no more to build a pretty car than an ugly one. The Jaguar 1½-Litre of 1938 (below) grew out of the same philosophy.

The founder of Jaguar, William Lyons, was born in Blackpool in 1901 and received his engineering training at the Crossley works and through evening classes at the Manchester Technical College. Subsequent events showed that it was clearly a sound training, even if it was not to an advanced level. Crossley, which vanished from the scene in 1937, is barely remembered today but it had a great tradition as one of the pioneers of the internal combustion engine – it had acquired rights to the original Otto engine as early as 1869.

Lyons returned home to Blackpool to work in the family piano restoring business and then took a job selling Sunbeam motorcycles while trading in motorcycles on his own after hours. Nothing in his early career suggested that Bill Lyons would become a giant of the motor industry...

Perhaps he would have remained in obscurity had not William Walmsley moved to a house near the Lyons family home and begun making light, pretty, aluminium-panelled sidecars which he sold under the name 'Swallow'. Lyons bought one, liked it, and was soon pestering Walmsley to go into partnership with him. Lyons knew that the product was good and, given the

right organisation, it could sell better than the one a week which Walmsley was able to make on his own.

Walmsley, who was ten years older, eventually agreed to join forces and on Lyons' 21st birthday, in September 1922, the Swallow Sidecar Company was formed thanks to the fathers of both men offering to guarantee a £1000 bank overdraft. The company prospered and in 1926 it changed its name to the Swallow Sidecar and Coachbuilding Company and moved to bigger premises. Here Lyons' twin talents came into their own: he was able to expand the business further and he began to style

An SS100 Jaguar from 1937 (above): was this 'Wardour Street Bentley' the best-looking sports car of its time? A less eye-catching, but still handsome, model in the SS range of the period was the 2½-Litre (left), available as a saloon or a tourer.

bodywork for cars. The first Swallow body, on an Austin Seven, appeared in 1927 and was an immediate success. Other special bodies followed, but production was restricted by the size of the factory, which permitted only two car bodies to be built alongside the 100 sidecars which were turned out each week.

Swallow moved to a former munitions factory in Coventry in 1929 and expansion continued. In 1930 the company was re-named the Swallow Coachbuilding Company and made its first appearance at the London Motor Show. By early 1931 Swallow was making 50 car

bodies a day, and Lyons was still only 28. He had shown himself to be a superb businessman and stylist, and this fuelled his ambitions. Despite the fact that the Depression was biting and famous marques were collapsing, he decided to build his own car. By that time relations between Lyons and Walmsley were becoming strained as the younger man became dominant.

Lyons took as his philosophy the idea that cars sold on their looks and that it was as cheap to build a handsome car as it was an ugly one – and the SS1 reflected that belief. When first shown at the London Motor Show in

A full-size styling model for Jaguar's new sports car was built in 1946, two years before the XK120's public launch. The shape is slightly more rounded and there are flanged creases along the top of the wings, but the XK theme has clearly been established.

1931 it was displayed without a price tag and the public was invited to guess how much it cost. It looked like a £1000 car, as many people guessed, but it actually cost just £310 and established a tradition of offering outstanding style for a fraction of what the opposition were asking.

While this was appreciated by some, who beat a path to Lyons' door, the cars were treated with disdain in some circles and 'Wardour Street Bentley' was one of the more polite labels applied to them – Wardour Street, in London's Soho, was then a centre of the entertainment industry in all of its expressions, legitimate and otherwise. The SS1 was considered flash, the sort of car which might be driven by a bookmaker or someone on the music halls, but there would come a time when the 'Wardour Street Bentley' would surpass the real Bentley's record at Le Mans.

There is no question, the SS1 was flash. With its long bonnet and low roof-line, it was the ultimate cad's car – you expected the driver to have a thin moustache and two-tone shoes. It was more show than go, however, because beneath the rakish body was the running gear from various side-valve Standard models (there were two engine options) and a special chassis made by Standard.

Lyons, a consummate showman, had the SS1 endorsed by a number of leading racing drivers, but its performance was unremarkable. However, his philosophy that cars sell on their looks was proved correct. In 1932 SS Cars sold 778 cars and the beauty was that it was a low-risk operation since all the expensive components

were bought in and the sidecar business provided a firm base for the company.

Other models followed and in January 1935 SS Cars Ltd was launched as a public company, at which point Walmsley left to make caravans (he died in 1961). Lyons became the largest shareholder in what was, notionally, a subsidiary of the Swallow Coachbuilding Company. Then Lyons put that company into voluntary liquidation and created a separate private company, Swallow Coachbuilding (1935) Ltd, which continued to make sidecars until the outbreak of war.

The sidecar company was later sold, and sold again, until in 1946 it came under the umbrella of Tube Investments (TI), whose diverse interests included the supply of door locks and bumpers to the motor industry. In 1954 TI decided to market a sports car to use up spare capacity at Swallow because the sidecar market was shrinking, and by then Swallow sidecars were not of the quality which had made the company's reputation. The Swallow Doretti used Triumph TR2 running gear in a chassis made of Reynolds 531 tubing (a TI product) and had a pretty aluminium body which bore some resemblance to the Austin-Healey 100.

It was always going to be a low-volume car, and although the Doretti has sometimes been dismissed as a failure, Swallow could not meet demand and 252 cars were made in 10 months before, with no public announcement, the model was withdrawn. Lyons had not been amused to find a supplier become a competitor, albeit a very small player, and despite the historical links

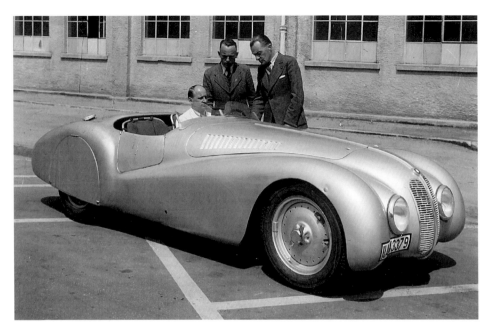

The XK120's styling was brilliant, but did other cars provide inspiration? The BMW sports-racer built for the 1940 Mille Miglia (left) and Paul Pycroft's special-bodied SS100 (below) may have been influences...

between Swallow and Jaguar, he issued TI with an ultimatum: either be a supplier or a competitor. The business with Jaguar was too lucrative to lose and so TI pulled the plug on the Doretti.

When Jaguar and Austin-Healey found themselves part of the same group in 1967, it was Lyons who was chiefly responsible for vetoing the proposed Austin-Healey 4000, a car which met the new American safety and emission laws. The trouble was that the Healey might have been a threat to the Jaguar E-type in America because it was cheaper and faster, and it had the cachet of a Rolls-Royce engine. For the same reason he also vetoed a promising mid-engined GT prototype built by Alvis. Lyons could be a hard man...

But these episodes lay in the future. The big advance of SS Cars came in 1935 when it commissioned Harry Weslake to design a pushrod overhead valve cylinder head for the sturdy Standard engine and took on William Heynes as chief engineer. Heynes' first job was to design a new crankshaft and lubrication system and the resulting engine formed the heart of a new range of cars known as 'SS Jaguar'. The name 'Jaguar' struck a chord with the public and although it was only a model title, it became the name by which SS was popularly known.

In 1936 came the overhead-valve 2½-litre SS100 Jaguar sports car, which was perhaps the most handsome production car of its era. Some people thought that the '100' indicated the car's top speed, but it stood for the 104bhp which the engine produced, its maximum speed being 92mph. That was still an exceptional figure for a

2½-litre unsupercharged car but, with tuning, the magic 'ton' could be reached.

Not many of these cars were made and their engineering could not be called sophisticated (they had beam front axles), but they looked gorgeous. The SS100 acted as the flagship to a successful range of sporting saloons and Lyons could not help but notice that the sports cars achieved a level of attention far beyond the modest numbers which were made.

The 125bhp 3½-litre SS100 of 1938 was capable of 104mph in standard trim and cost just £445, which was the most remarkable bargain Lyons had yet produced. It set the tone for the future: Jaguar would provide West End style and performance at East End prices. Only 110 examples of the 3½-litre SS100 were made, but it seemed more as privateers racked up many successes in competition. One SS100 lapped Brooklands at over 118mph, but the car was most at home in rallying and as

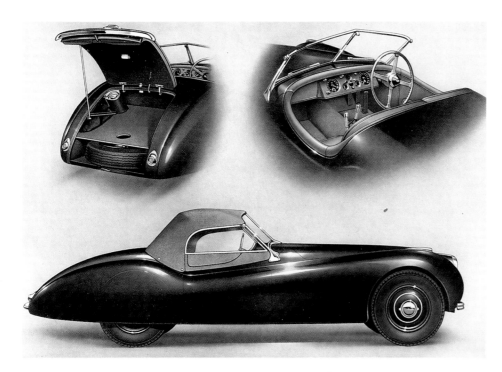

There is a little artistic licence in these studies from the first XK120 brochure, but they capture the beauty of the new Jaguar's lines.

late as 1948 Ian Appleyard won the Alpine Rally in one.

In 1939 the Jaguar factory was turned over to war work and senior management took their part in fire-watching duties. At times they were extremely busy since Coventry was hit hard by the Luftwaffe, but in the latter stages of the war these mandatory duties turned into brain-storming sessions as they planned the future. Apart from Lyons, the senior engineers at these meetings were William Heynes, Claude Baily and Walter Hassan.

Many proposals were aired and several engine design studies were undertaken, each with the designation 'X' (for 'experimental'). While early proposals (XA, XB, etc) did not proceed beyond initial drawings, the XF was built. It was a double overhead camshaft four-cylinder unit of 1360cc which was built primarily to assess a twin camshaft crossflow engine, but the block was considered inadequate. The XG was based on a 1776cc Standard engine with a cylinder head which followed BMW 328 practice, but it was not sufficiently powerful or sophisticated for Jaguar's future requirements.

Then came the XJ, a double overhead camshaft unit designed to be built with four cylinders or six, and this remained 'warm' for some years. Indeed, when the XK120 was announced, it was stated that an XK100 model using a 2-litre four-cylinder XJ engine would also be available. A 146bhp version, which was close to standard specification, was installed in 'Goldie' Gardner's ex-MG record-breaking special in 1948 and powered the

car to 176.96mph on the Jabbeke highway in Belgium. Apparently the XK100 was mooted to make maximum capital of this achievement, but the engine never achieved sufficient levels of refinement to be signed off for production.

For years the XK100 engine figured in the fantasies of British racing car makers because it was potentially far superior to the Bristol unit which was the usual, enforced, choice of British constructors. Had Jaguar had been a little more generous and released a batch of XJ engines, the history of British motor racing might have been significantly different.

A six-cylinder XJ engine of 3182cc was built, but it was felt that it produced insufficient torque. By increasing the stroke, however, this obstacle was overcome and led to the 3442cc double overhead camshaft XK engine, which was earmarked for a saloon that was intended to be a Bentley rival. It was an inspired decision, but also a gamble. Nobody knew what conditions would be like after the war and many people advocated small economical cars for the masses. For a company with only eight years of car production behind it, such a car was a bold step. The gas-flow specialist, Harry Weslake, was engaged as a consultant on the new engine.

One thing which influenced the final design was that Standard informed Lyons it would be unable to supply him with engines after the war because it had no plans to revive the models on which Jaguar based its engines.

THE JAGUAR XK SUPER SPORTS TWO-SEATER

Lyons promptly bought Standard's machine tooling and one of the constraints of the XK engine was that it had to be made using this tooling.

During the war, the initials 'SS' had acquired unfortunate connotations, so in 1945 the company became Jaguar Cars Ltd. It revived some of its pre-war range, but restrictions on materials and even electricity delayed production of the car which would become the MkVII saloon. The broad outlines of the chassis were incorporated into the MkV saloon, which had the now-familiar twin-wishbone and torsion bar independent front suspension, but it retained the Standard engine with the Jaguar overhead-valve conversion.

When it became apparent that the MkVII would not appear until about 1951, Lyons became worried. He needed a car to drum up interest and so decided to build a sports model to display at the 1948 London Motor Show. Jaguar had the XK engine but no car to put it in, so he decided to 'cut-and-shut' a MkV chassis and put an aluminium and ash body on top.

Many stories have accrued around the prototype XK120, or the 'Open Two-Seater Super Sports' as it was initially billed – but the 'SS' part of the designation was soon dropped and 'OTS' did not catch on either. Henceforth, we shall call the prototype's body configuration by the name it came to be known in retrospect, as the 'Roadster'.

Lyons developed the body style in his usual way,

First put into production with an aluminium body mounted on an ash frame, the XK was given the cumbersome title of 'Super Sports Two-Seater'. The earliest aluminium cars had straight windscreen pillars, as seen here.

having craftsmen make panels which were painted and attached to a buck. It took him just two weeks to finalise the shape, which was so absolutely right that only detail modifications were made for the production cars. Two weeks is an astonishingly short time, but Lyons had been thinking along similar lines for some time and in 1946-47 he had made a mock-up of a body style that contained many of the XK120's key elements.

Lyons felt that he might possibly sell 200 cars, and since they would be in the hands of sports car enthusiasts he would obtain useful feedback for the design of the MkVII, which remained Jaguar's chief priority. A cynic might judge that 200 buyers were to be used as guinea pigs at their own expense, except that in the event each received the bargain of the century.

It is worth noting that several specialist coachbuilders essayed styles on XK120 and XK140 chassis, among them Ghia and Pinin Farina (later Pininfarina). They were greeted with respectful interest, but nobody ever said that they were a patch on the original. When it came to styling, Lyons was a genius and it is a shame that he has never received the credit he deserves as one of the greatest stylists in automotive history.

Jaguar's initial publicity promised a 2-litre 'XK100' (above left). The car never reached production, but the four-cylinder 146bhp engine did exist and was installed in a streamlined MG record-breaker (above). 'Goldie' Gardner (white helmet), who reached 176mph in this MG, chats to Jaguar engineer Wally Hassan.

The XK120 was unveiled in October 1948 and it set the automotive world back on its heels. At this distance it is hard to imagine the impact it had, but let us put it in context. In Britain in 1948 even the most basic commodities were still rationed – you could not buy a pair of trousers without either clothing coupons or a contact on the black market. Unless there were special medical reasons, each adult could buy only one fresh egg a week and to buy meat you had to register with a butcher. There had been epidemics of polio and whooping cough. People who lived in large cities were used to 'pea soup' fogs. London was littered with bomb sites, but in the rest of Europe some towns were bomb sites with a few buildings. In some countries reprisals were still being carried out against people who had collaborated during the war or who had backed the wrong side. When people talked about dealing in drugs they meant medicines such as penicillin.

Into this monochrome world the XK120 was sprung upon the motoring public like Rita Hayworth in an all-singing, all-dancing, Technicolor showcase number from an MGM musical inserted into one of those black and white films where detectives wore trilbies and trench coats and drove around in Wolseleys with bells on the front. It was sensational – nothing less – and when the news spread that the '120' designation referred to its top speed, it became an icon.

One hundred and twenty miles an hour made the XK120 the fastest unsupercharged sports car in the world, ever, and here it was being offered for sale. Jaguar's vague plans to make a couple of hundred cars turned into an initial run of 240 with aluminium and ash bodies – but the response took everyone by surprise. The future had arrived and the most beautiful car in the world could be yours for a staggeringly low basic price of £998.

That was the theory, but in fact the government had rationed the supply of materials and car makers had to agree to export at least 50 per cent of their output. That led to a remarkable situation in 1950, when Britain exported more cars than every other country in the world combined. Jaguar had hardly sold any cars abroad in the 1930s, save for a few which went to the Commonwealth, but the company's exports during the 1950s would peak at over 90 per cent of production, with the bulk going to North America.

The British customer who turned up for the 1948 Motor Show had no chance of buying an XK120, even if he had the money. At the time you put your name down on a waiting list for your preferred model and even such unglamorous cars as the Morris Oxford had a six-year waiting list. When the great day came and you took delivery of your car, which was invariably painted black, you had to sign a covenant agreeing not to sell it for at least a year because moving it on so soon, probably at a hefty premium, was seen as 'black marketeering'.

The XK120's claimed top speed seemed so extraordinary in 1948 that it was widely doubted until the following year, when the works tester, Ron 'Soapy' Sutton, took a car to Jabbeke, regularly exceeding 130mph and recording a best of 132.6mph. For that run the car was fitted with a metal cowl around the cockpit, but Sutton achieved 126mph with full weather equipment in place. For many of the journalists who had

Jaguar's other models are still under wraps at the 1948 Earls Court Motor Show, but the fantastic new XK already has admirers.

been taken to Belgium by Dakota, it was equally remarkable that 'Soapy' was then able to drive past at 10mph in top gear. One magazine later recorded a 0-100mph time of 44sec – in top gear! No other production car of the time was capable of going from zero to over 120mph in the same gear.

The XK120's styling was the main talking point because it was quite unlike anything which had come from Britain before. At a time when British sports cars usually had cycle wings and large headlights, it was as sleek and lithe as a cat. And in styling terms it was perhaps the first international car to come from a British manufacturer.

There have been many suggestions about the origins of the styling. Some have supported the claims of Paul Pycroft (who financed the Costin 'Amigo') that it was inspired by a special body which he had fitted to his SS100, although this car was ugly and ill-proportioned by comparison. One can certainly see the genesis of the XK120 in some of the bodywork made by French and Italian coachbuilders in the late 1930s. When the Fixed-Head Coupé came along in 1951, there was no mistaking its antecedents because the roof-line followed that of a styling exercise which Lyons himself had made on an SS100 in 1938.

If there must be a direct inspiration, it is one of the BMW 328s which BMW built for the 1940 Gran Premio di Brescia della Mille Miglia. This race is often claimed to

have been a Mille Miglia, but it was not. It merely incorporated 'Mille Miglia' in its title and it was run over nine laps of a 103-mile course and not over a single lap of Italy. One of the special BMWs was appropriated by H.J.Aldington (of AFN, the pre-war British BMW importer) and was fitted with a Frazer Nash radiator grille with the idea that it might become a production model. Nothing came of that, but Lyons saw the car and was impressed. Photographs do not do justice to the BMW, but when it is seen in three dimensions its influence on Lyons' styling exercise of 1946-47, and hence on the XK120, is apparent.

The BMW remains, however, only an influence because the XK120 was a unique machine with its long, flowing bonnet and exquisite radiator grille. Psychologists could have a field day contemplating that long bonnet and the shape of that grille. If the XK120 was nothing else, it was sexy.

At a time of 'Export or Die', the original limited production run went by the board and the design was re-engineered with a steel body. This delayed volume production by a year but ultimately allowed Jaguar to sell 12,055 XK120s. People are always prepared to suffer for style so owners endured the cramped cockpit, poor gearchange and brakes, and all the other snags. If the frock looks great, who cares if you can't run for a bus in it? Actually, if the frock is that good you never have to travel by bus.

THE RANGE IN BRIEF

There are three main strands to consider when looking at the XK series. The first is that the XK120 was only intended as a stunt to drum up publicity for the MkVII saloon. The second is that with a production car capable of over 120mph, Jaguar was entering uncharted waters. Specialist makers of hand-built cars were proud if they could claim that their products were capable of the 'ton', let alone 120mph, a level of performance previously achieved only by a handful of supercharged machines. Finally, the inter-action between the company's competition programme and its road models was unique for a mass-produced car.

The reception of the XK120 'Open Two Seater Super Sports' took Jaguar by surprise. It had arranged a supply of aluminium panels from J.H.Cooke & Sons of Nottingham and ash frames from another source, but

Cutaway doors and the short cockpit instantly distinguish this XK120 as the Roadster or 'Open Two Seater' version, the first of three body designs that became available by 1953.

these were the components of a hand-built car and even a year after the XK120's announcement few had been delivered. Lyons then committed himself to making the car a full-blown production model and commissioned Pressed Steel Ltd to supply steel bodies. It was not until May 1950 that these came on stream, by which time the company had made 240 'lightweights'. Although five of the original six quasi-works competition cars were supplied to British drivers, no aluminium-bodied car was actually sold through a dealer in Britain.

Production cars differed only in detail from the

Two other body styles were launched during the XK120's life, and continued for the XK140 and XK150 updates. The Fixed-Head Coupé (left) arrived in 1951, and the Drophead Coupé (below) followed in 1953.

prototype. They had a slightly higher front bumper and cooling vents appeared below it. At the back the prototype had a low, horizontal, one-piece bumper similar in style to the front one, and the rear lights and the number plate were set low.

The success of the new car – and of the MkVII that arrived in 1951 – meant that Jaguar had to find new factory space, and the company was also to buy obsolete production lines from Standard. These were expedients, within a tight budget, but while they allowed Jaguar to expand production beyond anything previously dreamed of, they were later to contribute to the company's mid-life crisis. They simply did not allow the workforce to make significant productivity improvements.

There was a fundamental problem with the XK120: while Jaguar had made perhaps the largest single leap

with a power unit in the history of the production car, many of the other major components did not match its standard. It is one thing to be able to do 120mph, but another to be able to see the road if you are doing it at night and yet another if you need to stop from that speed. In both areas, the original XK120 was deficient.

These flaws were not a case of incompetence on the part of Jaguar, but of the unavailability of suitable components. The XK120's 12in drum brakes were the largest that would fit practically with 16in wheels, but they overheated when stressed because it was not possible to cool them adequately despite vents under the front bumper. This was partly due to the enveloping bodywork and partly because Jaguar had to fit pressed steel wheels – nobody was making 16in 'wires' at a reasonable price.

15

Spot the difference. The overall shape has the same flavour, but compared with its predecessor the XK140 Fixed-Head Coupé has more height and length to its cabin. Brochure illustration (facing page) shows two XK140 recognition points – more robust bumpers and a cast grille with fewer slats.

Borrani could have supplied them, but £300 for a set of five sat uneasily on a £998 car. It has been suggested that it was the clout of BMC (and a ten-year contract) when it put the Austin-Healey 100 into production which persuaded Dunlop to relent and the XK120 tagged along on the Healey's coat-tails. In fact, Jaguar had formed a close relationship with Dunlop – they were to develop a disc brake system together – and 54-spoke Dunlop wire wheels were standard on the Special Equipment model which arrived in March 1951, when the Austin-Healey was not even a twinkle in Donald Healey's eye. Besides, the Healey had 48-spoke wheels until the initial contract with Dunlop expired and it could finally fit 60-spoke wheels.

The Moss gearbox was never an XK's main attraction, but it was the only proprietary unit capable of handling 160bhp and more. Jaguar had done well to advance from being a coachbuilder to becoming an established marque in a few years – it must be the only surviving maker to have done that – and it did not have the capacity to create everything in-house. When the XK120 first appeared there was so much to admire that the gearbox was accepted, but as the car became more familiar it received more attention from road testers.

Jaguar also had insufficient experience of building a car capable of such speed, but then the only firms with this ability had years of motor racing behind them. Jaguar was pioneering a new concept in production cars and

naturally it made mistakes, but it had a very rapid response time and the XK series continued to receive improvements throughout its life. Jaguar's competition programme revealed other shortcomings in the early cars which were not apparent during normal testing, and motor racing really did help improve the breed.

The competition cars are an integral part of the XK story since they were all based on standard (or prototype) components. Disc braking is the most famous example, but the competition programme also evaluated fuel injection at a time when it was virtually unknown to the world at large and, of course, the E-type was a production edition of the D-type.

At first the XK120 Super Sports was supplied as a traditional British sports car, with cutaway doors (without external handles), side-screens and a stowaway hood. This configuration was re-named the 'Roadster' when the Fixed-Head Coupé was announced in March 1951. At the same time a version with a tuned 180bhp engine, wire wheels and other refinements was known as the Special Equipment or, unofficially, as the XK120M (M for 'Modified') in North America.

Finally, in 1953, came the Drophead Coupé, which had a fixed hood and wind-up windows. Thus was established the pattern for the future of the steel-bodied cars: there would be three body styles but the Roadster would be the most popular until late in the range's life.

The C-type, originally the XK120C, was also put on

sale in 'production' form in 1953. Its availability was part of Jaguar's overall strategy because using the jigs and body formers spread the cost of building the cars which the works ran in competition. You could order one from your local Jaguar dealer and, since most of the mechanical parts were shared with the road cars, your dealer could maintain it. It was the McLaren F1 of its day.

In late 1954 the XK120 was replaced by the XK140, in essence a MkII version. The body remained virtually unchanged in outward appearance but the cockpit was enlarged by moving the engine, scuttle and windscreen forward by 3in, which meant that few panels were interchangeable with the XK120. In the Fixed-Head Coupé and Drophead Coupé there were token seats which were suitable for small children for short journeys, but these were little more than slim excuses for the first generation of customers to buy one. A guy with an early XK120 was likely to have ensnared the High School Prom Queen and, by 1954, was looking for extra seats.

The XK140's main identification features were a cast grille with fewer bars and fairly beefy bumpers in place of the original versions, which were aesthetically pleasing but inadequate as bumpers. Since most cars went Stateside, where motorists often had a robust attitude to parking, the bumpers were necessary, but some people thought that the range had gone soft.

Times had changed and the XK was no longer at the leading edge of competition, but the Roadster (without the 'Plus Two' seats) remained the most popular version. A power increase to 190bhp as standard or 210bhp for the Special Equipment cars made up for the XK140's slight gain in weight, and the range benefited from much more positive rack and pinion steering. There were improvements all round apart from ultimate aesthetics – but it was still possible to buy an XK120 radiator grille and bumpers if you desperately needed them.

By 1954, however, the XK series had a different place in the scheme of things. The Mercedes-Benz 300SL 'gullwing' had become the most exciting production car in the world, and the fastest. No longer could one say that the XK was the most beautiful car in the world – some designs from coachbuilders in Italy surpassed it, not to mention cars from Austin-Healey and Aston Martin.

The XK140 still offered matchless value, but it had become a mass-produced sports car rather than a phenomenon. It sat in the market ahead of the Chevrolet Corvette and Austin-Healey 100 in terms of performance, but many people would argue that the Healey, which was cheaper, had greater 'kerb presence'. On the other hand, the Healey did not have a badge on the boot recording the company's victories at Le Mans.

At the 1954 London Motor Show Jaguar offered the D-type as a production car. Unlike the C-type, which was sometimes bought solely for road use, this was a racing car which was also road-legal, but then World Sports Car Championship regulations made that a

The XK150 appeared first in Drophead and Fixed-Head forms, the Roadster arriving 10 months later – here it is on its public debut at the New York Motor Show in April 1958.

minimum requirement. D-types could be, and were, driven to circuits, but a partition between the driver and passenger made it a road car of marginal practicality.

That was changed early in 1957 when, concerned by the quantity of D-type components piled up in the warehouse, Jaguar made the XKSS. It seems hardly credible that the D-type did not find a wider market at the price until you look at the production figures for the Ford GT40 and the Lancia Stratos. Three of the greatest cars, and the greatest bargains, in motoring history, yet between them they sold fewer than 200 units. Too late people realised what they had missed, which is why makers of replicas have since had a field day.

The XKSS was an open-cockpit, short-nose D-type with a fixed hood, bumpers, brightwork, a full-size glass windscreen with wipers, and a luggage rack on the rear panel. It was aimed particularly at the American market, where it could compete in SCCA racing as a production model. Only 16 were made before the fire at the Jaguar works destroyed most of the surplus components and production ended.

A few months later came the XK150, which was a further improvement over the staple series although many people saw it as an overweight, decadent parody of the XK120. That was an unfair perception because the XK150 was roomier, better equipped and virtually all cars had four-wheel disc brakes although, officially, these were optional on the base model. It retained the overall style of the XK120, but had smoother lines and a curved, one-piece windscreen. Jaguar clearly saw it in a slightly different light from earlier cars because it was offered at first only in Fixed-Head Coupé and Drophead Coupé versions, the Roadster (with wind-up windows) not

appearing until March 1958. At the same time a 250bhp 'S' engine was an option across the range.

Even though production would cease before the end of 1960 (the last XK sold in Britain was delivered in November) to prepare for the E-type, Jaguar continued to improve the range. In October 1959 it offered a 220bhp 3.8-litre engine with a 265bhp 'S' option which was capable of 136mph. In 11 years of production life the XK engine had improved from 160bhp to 265bhp, which was more than either the Mercedes-Benz 300SL Roadster or the Ferrari 250GT could offer – and you could buy three Jaguars for the price of a Ferrari.

Despite this staggering performance, highly developed chassis and four-wheel disc brakes, the public perceived the XK series differently in the late 1950s – the Fixed-Head Coupé was easily the most popular version of the XK150 and many owners specified the optional Borg Warner automatic transmission. Behind Jaguar had come a number of cheaper sports cars which appealed to young bloods and the XK150 was seen more as a Grand Tourer, but this assessment was not altogether fair.

In real motoring terms, driving from A to B on a winding route, the XK150 'S' was one of the best sports cars in the world. Few could match it for outright performance, none could match its braking, and it handled superbly. Its style was perhaps a little dated, but it had refinement and was still the best value for money on the sports car market. Some people believe that it was superior in some areas to the E-type which replaced it.

Perhaps the XK line had been around so long that people were no longer startled by it as they had been when the XK120 made its debut. That was to change in March 1961 when Jaguar unveiled the E-type.

THE XK120

The XK120's announcement took the world completely by surprise. There had been no carefully orchestrated 'scoop' pictures in the press so its impact was the greater. For many people in Britain the fact that the Motor Show was staged in 1948 was a welcome sign that things were returning to normal, but nobody expected sensation.

This was a time before the 'dream cars' which would become a feature of American motor shows of the 1950s, or the 'concept cars' which are regularly seen today. The average person would have expected the majority of exhibits to be familiar and what mild surprises there might be would be found on the stands of the specialist makers such as Healey or in the coachbuilding section. It was enough to be able to attend a motor show again and dream how things might be at some time in the future when things returned to normal. The XK120 gave everyone a new standard in fantasy and it also had a profound influence on the styling of many sports cars of the 1950s.

It had no rivals for performance, price or style. Aston Martin was exhibiting what, in retrospect, would be called the DB1, but that hardly took the world by storm. Allard was making robust, simple, Ford-engined specials without a compound curve in their bodies, while Healey offered a range of fast, elegant cars for the wealthy few. With the exception of Morris and its new Minor,

Relatively simple construction lies beneath the XK120's skin: a conventional chassis derived from the MkV, a live axle rear end and double wishbone front suspension.

virtually all other makers had lightly revised pre-war models on their stands.

If this was the state of things in Britain, elsewhere in Europe the situation was even worse. Of the makers which were, or would become, Jaguar's rivals, Alfa Romeo was still struggling to get a post-war car into production and Porsche was building its first VW-based special. Ferrari had yet to make a road car, BMW's factory was stranded in the Russian zone of Germany and it would not make cars in Munich until late 1952, while Mercedes-Benz production was running at less than a fifth of its pre-war rate.

The great French constructors struggled with pre-war – and very expensive – designs, but conditions in France meant that their market had all but disappeared. Even those who could afford to buy a new Delahaye or Bugatti felt it politic not to do so since the possession of such apparent wealth could carry with it the suspicion that one had been a collaborator during the German occupation, or was now a black marketeer.

Residual bitterness from the war years made for dangerous times in many European countries. The

impact of the XK120 was the greater for it having no rivals, but above all else it symbolised a better future and after nearly ten years of darkness people desperately needed to believe in that.

The heart of the XK series was the engine – a thing of beauty in itself. In the uncluttered engine bay sat a magnificent lump of metal with a bright aluminium alloy cylinder head which was known to be ready for mass production – and its beauty was not accidental. In a paper delivered to the Institute of Mechanical Engineers in 1953, William Heynes said: "There was just one more requirement which had to be met – one which automobile engineers (on both sides of the Atlantic) as a general rule ignore – and that is the styling of the external design of the engine so that it looks the high-efficiency unit it is". One wonders how much Heynes had been influenced by William Lyons' maxim that it is as cheap to build a handsome car as an ugly one.

In the manner of the day, the 3442cc XK engine was relatively long-stroked and slow revving, with an 83mm bore, a 106mm stroke and a 7:1 compression ratio. This

Slender bumpers and a radiator grille with thin slats identify this car as an XK120, and the simple windscreen frame pinpoints it as a Roadster.

fairly low compression ratio was dictated by the poor quality of the fuel then available – typically around 72 octane. As we have seen, Jaguar wanted an engine with plenty of torque and that meant a long-stroke engine – and in any case long-stroke engines were ingrained in the culture of the British motor industry.

Until 1948 cars in Britain were taxed according to a notional 'horsepower' formula devised many years earlier. Manufacturers of popular cars bore this in mind and the formula encouraged four-cylinder long-stroke engines – a Ford V8 Pilot saloon rated at 30hp attracted more tax than a four-cylinder 4.5-litre supercharged Bentley rated at 18hp. Jaguar had already finalised its XK engine by the time a flat-rate car tax of £10 per year was introduced.

With two 1.75in SU H6 carburettors, the XK engine delivered 160bhp at 5000rpm and 195lb ft of torque at 2500rpm, but it was obvious that this was just the

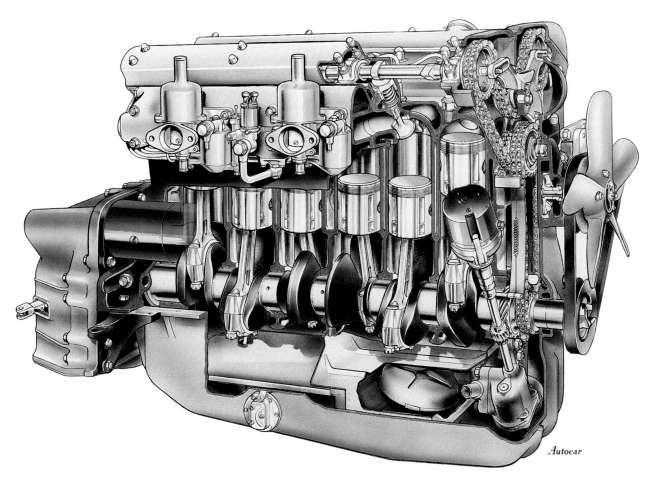

Autocar

beginning and that much more power could be obtained with tuning. In the early 1960s a factory-prepared, fuel-injected, 3.8-litre XK engine developed for John Coombs' Lightweight E-type would produce 345bhp.

At the time most garage mechanics had never seen a double overhead camshaft engine, let alone worked on one, but this had been taken care of in the design. There was nothing complicated about the XK engine and any competent mechanic could take one apart and reassemble it from experience alone. This helps to explain why the XK engine remained in production until 1986, about 20 years longer than the most optimistic forecast when the unit first appeared.

The valves were set at 70 degrees to create a hemispherical head with the sparking plugs top centre. The camshafts were driven by duplex chains and acted through floating tappets, which reduced the unsprung weight of the valve gear and allowed relatively light valve springs, creating a more free-revving engine. The seven crankshaft bearings were unusually large at 2.75in in diameter, but they gave the crankshaft exceptional

The XK engine, a twin overhead camshaft design that was way ahead of its time, in a cutaway study and under the bonnet of an XK120.

JWK 675 was *The Autocar*'s test car in 1951 – the fact that Jaguar issued a British magazine with a left-hand drive car shows how the company was building almost solely for export in the early years. The Roadster's hood and sidescreens are rather inelegant when erected.

Journalists gather round a right-hand drive Roadster (the lack of front wing air vents shows it is an early one) during a factory visit. The car's brightwork has been masked up for protection on the journey to its buyer.

rigidity and allowed the engine to reach maximum revs with remarkable smoothness. The XK engine won Le Mans five times, but it also enabled Daimler Limousines to move sedately and silently in funeral processions.

Although the XK was a glimpse into the future, it was still an engine of its time and all XK units would have relatively heavy oil consumption by modern standards. On early versions there was a problem with oil leaking from the camshaft covers, but this was fixed in November 1951 by adding extra studs to the head. Another indication that it was a car of its time was the fact that the first 26 delivered were equipped with starting handles.

The engine drove through a 10in Borg & Beck single-plate clutch and a four-speed Moss gearbox with synchromesh on the top three ratios. The 'box tended to be tolerated rather than admired, but it was the only proprietary unit which would take the engine's power and Jaguar was not a large enough company to develop

its own transmission system. In fact, the Moss gearbox was not a bad unit by the standards of the day, and only later were reservations expressed about it.

The XK120's chassis was simple, a 'cut-and-shut' version of the chassis used for the Jaguar MkV saloon, but with the wheelbase reduced to 102in. It was a very stiff structure consisting of two shallow box-section side-members, with box-section central cross-bracing which kicked up at the rear. There was further cross-bracing ahead of and behind the fuel tank, which was located ahead of the boot and which, in rough terms, extended from the rear axle line to a line drawn between the rearmost extremity of the rear wheels. Two six-volt batteries were mounted in tandem behind the seats.

Front suspension was by double wishbones with 52in longitudinal torsion bars, telescopic dampers and an anti-roll bar mounted in rubber bushes. Rear suspension was by live axle, semi-elliptical seven-leaf springs and Girling lever-arm shock absorbers. Lockheed hydraulic brakes

132·6 M.P.H. ON PUMP PETROL . . .

On May 10th, 1949, an entirely standard Jaguar 3½ litre XK 120 Sports Two-Seater, running on pump fuel, attained a speed of 112.6 m.p.h. over a flying mile on the Jabbeke-Aeltre Road in Belgium. This speed was officially timed by the Royal Automobile Club of Belgium and is the fastest ever recorded by a standard production unsupercharged car.

Jaguar boasted about Ron 'Soapy' Sutton's sensational speed run in the XK120 catalogue (right) and on a dashboard plaque fitted to export Roadsters (below).

CERTIFIED
THAT THIS JAGUAR CAR IS AN
EXACT REPLICA
OF THE RECORD-BREAKING CAR
WHICH ACHIEVED THE SPEED OF
132.6 M.P.H.
AT JABBEKE, BELGIUM, 30 MAY, 1949
CERTIFIED BY
CHIEF ENGINEER
JAGUAR CARS LTD., COVENTRY ENGLAND

with two leading shoes and 12in drums were fitted all round. The chassis was the epitome of simplicity, yet it worked well under most conditions – although one would have to be totally besotted to pretend that the roadholding was perfect.

As it happens, most new owners were besotted and were prepared to accept the car's shortcomings, which included marginal cooling in heavy traffic and brakes that were somewhat less than perfect. Customers wanted the styling and the kudos of a car which would achieve a genuine 120mph, although how many actually drove at that speed is another matter entirely. The vast majority of cars anyway went to the USA and it is not being rude to say that, at the time, most Americans did not have high expectations of roadholding and brakes.

Only minor changes to the body were made between the prototype and the first batch of 240 aluminium-bodied cars, and the only differences between these and the steel-bodied versions were subtle ones which basically arose from the fact that the aluminium cars were hand-built. The two most visible distinctions were that the aluminium cars had slight curvature on the detachable spats over the rear wheels (they were flat on the steel cars) and the attaching brackets to the rear bumpers were colour-keyed with the bodywork (they tended to be black on the steel cars). Another detail difference was that the aluminium cars had larger rubber grommets under the windscreen frame in order to absorb the weight of the hood and to prevent the lighter metal from buckling. The windscreen itself was detachable on all XK120 Roadsters and for sportier owners an aero screen was included in the list of options.

It is an over-simplification to refer to 'aluminium' and 'steel' cars when dealing with the XK120 since all had aluminium doors, bonnets and boot lids, but the first batch were all-aluminium and were constructed on ash frames. One also has to take the pragmatic view that since so many XK120s of both types have undergone restoration, one cannot be dogmatic about what one may see on an individual car today.

Since the steel cars weighed 2970lb, about 100lb heavier than the aluminium batch, one would not expect them to be quite as swift, but there were some glaring anomalies in performance figures and they must be treated with caution. Most people settle for a top speed of at least 120mph with 0-60mph in 10sec, but road testing was, to put it mildly, an inexact art and it was not unknown for manufacturers to provide magazines with specially prepared cars.

In the case of the XK120 it would seem that at least some record attempts were undertaken when the car was fitted with optional extras such as a detachable undertray, which appeared on the options list but was rarely fitted to production cars. Still, this allowed Jaguar to claim that its records had been set by production cars and many early cars bore a plaque stating that an identical model had achieved 132.6mph – today such claims might be scrutinised by regulators of advertising standards.

When *The Autocar* tested a steel-bodied XK120 it could cover 0-60mph in no better than 12sec, and made no attempt to set a maximum speed. Using a 'lightweight', *The Motor* had achieved 124.6mph and covered 0-60mph in 9.9sec. Some road testers simply accepted Jaguar's record runs as the maximum speed since they had nowhere to attempt to emulate them, but others believed that the true top speed of a steel car was nearer 110mph than 120mph.

The matter is further complicated by the fact that Jaguar did not lend cars for testing on a regular basis – no XK140 was ever tested in a British magazine and the XK140 evaluated by American magazines had the full list of engine options. Build quality was also less consistent than it is today and the way that a car was run-in played a crucial part, so the performance of individual cars could vary significantly. Things became really complicated when overdrive and different rear axle ratios were

Few cars look as exquisite as an XK120 Roadster – the vent flap on the front wing shows this one was built after November 1951. Cars with steel disc wheels had rear spats (below).

offered, but a rough rule of thumb is that the Fixed-Head Coupé had a slightly higher top speed, while the Roadster was fastest over the 0-60mph sprint.

I have already alluded to some of the XK120's shortcomings: it is undeniable that the headlights and brakes were not adequate, but no suppliers had ever had to cope before with such performance in a production car. It is to Jaguar's lasting credit that through a

Compared with XK140, first XK has simple overriders and a full-depth boot lid. Roadster interior shows bench-like seats and a dashboard layout of classical simplicity.

thoughtful, rather than vigorous, competition programme, it addressed the problems. Although Jaguar was by no means the first company to use disc brakes, it played a larger part in their development than any other car manufacturer.

While one may understand why some aspects of the car were not perfect, others were less forgiveable – and one such was the seating. At first sight the seats could be mistaken for a bench with individually-moulded back supports. Closer examination showed that each side had fore/aft adjustment (it is typical of the car that the adjusting handle was chromed) and there was a padded section between the seats. This arrangement would have been acceptable on a luxury tourer, but was inadequate for high-speed motoring. Jaguar admitted as much when it later made bucket seats available as an optional extra. On the other hand, few of the cars were ever used to their maximum potential and one does not need competition seats when cruising a boulevard wearing a white suit, fedora and shades.

Cockpit space was another matter. By today's standards the cabin was cramped and the 17in Bluemels

The rich and famous bought XKs. Film actor Tyrone Power had his Roadster fitted with a Fox & Nicholl detachable hard-top.

steering wheel was too close to the driver. By the standards of its time, however, the XK120's driving position was acceptable and in line with most other sports cars – and an adjustable steering column was fitted in 1951. The arms' length driving style, pioneered by Dr Giuseppe Farina, the first World Champion, had not then come into fashion and drivers were used to hunching over the wheel. It is still something, however, which requires adjustment for most modern drivers.

The rest of the ergonomics were excellent. The gear lever and 'fly-off' handbrake 'fell easily to the hand', as road testers used to say, and the dashboard layout was exemplary. The dashboard was covered in leather with the instrument console standing proud and angled slightly upwards so that it could be seen more easily. The tachometer was red-lined at 5500rpm and incorporated a clock, while on the other side of the console the speedometer was calibrated to 140mph. Schoolboys would gather around a parked XK120 and gape at that speedometer.

Mounted in a triangle between the main instruments were three smaller dials. The base of the triangle was formed by an ammeter and a fuel gauge, the latter doubling until October 1952 as an oil level gauge (by pressing a button you could obtain a reading of how much oil was in the sump). At the apex of the triangle was a combined oil pressure and water temperature gauge, and in its centre was a twist switch for the lights. Other items such as the ignition switch, push-button starter, cigar lighter and warning lights were neatly arranged and all in plain sight. The layout was a model of neatness and clarity, and no car's dashboard at the time, not even a Bentley's, was better equipped.

An 'air conditioning unit' (actually a rather inefficient heater) was an option before becoming standard in November 1951, although the unit fitted to the Roadster did not have a demist function until the following year. A Radiomobile wireless was an optional extra, and no XK-series car had a radio as standard.

Since the priority of the designers had been to serve the driver as well as possible, the instrument panel left no room for a glove compartment, but the remaining space was occupied by a chromed grab handle. There was padding all round the top of the cockpit and the rear-view mirror was mounted on top of the scuttle.

Behind the seats was stowed the hood, which had proper internal bracing in contrast to the crude 'sticks and canvas' affairs of so many contemporary sports cars. The hood frame was complicated, chromed, and a minor work of art. From 1951 the catches on top of the

Speed that's made Jaguar a winner in over 46 major races . . . a *lifesaver* in modern American traffic!

Hill Power that wins the most famous international rallies.

Just for the fun of it!

XK 120 Super Sports priced from $3245 at Port of Entry Wire wheels and white wall tires additional

Maneuverability for *any* road situation!

A highly personal car . . . for those who appreciate superior motoring performance! Jaguar's famed engine makes it the world's *fastest* stock car. Low center of gravity, precision steering and braking power—the *safest*. Superb "roadability"—*the most exciting!* Let your dealer show you Jaguar in action . . . *just for the fun of it!*

Braking Power from oversized racing brakes—for quick, abrupt stops!

JAGUAR
the finest car of its class in the world

Importer West of the Mississippi • THE HOFFMAN MOT

CHARLES H. HORNBURG, Jr., INC., 9176 SUNSET BLVD., LOS ANGELES

Advert from *Road & Track* magazine tempts the all-important American market – 85 per cent of XK120s were exported.

windscreen were adjustable so that the hood could be tensioned. The rear window, however, was small and on early cars was placed so low that it was virtually useless.

With the detachable sidescreens in place, visibility was further impaired because the 'clear' area was reduced in size in order to incorporate lower hinged panels through which the driver could stick his arm to execute hand signals. These hinged panels were also required to gain access to the car by pulling on the cord inside either door – no external door handles were not fitted to what, in retrospect, became the Roadster. Not long into the production run of the steel cars, internal locks were

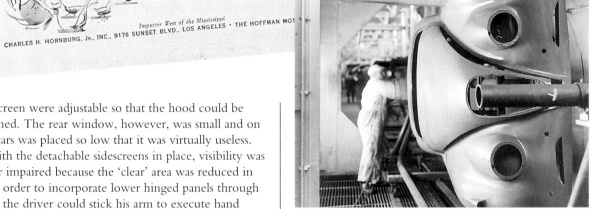

Special jigs rotated XK bodyshells as they passed through Jaguar's paintshop at Browns Lane. This XK120

Roadster's sidelight housings are integral with the front wings, indicating that it was built after October 1952.

added in the form of an extra knob which one twisted on the inside of each door.

On early cars there were no door stops, which meant that care had to be exercised in case a door swung forwards and hit the front wing. It was typical of Jaguar that throughout the car's production life small details like this were addressed. Some cockpit storage space was available in the gap between the door's inner panel and the outer skin, and this area was covered by a flap secured by studs at the bottom. Many manufacturers were content to leave a hole in the door panel, but such details were typical – West End quality at an East End price.

Boot space was not vast, although a two-piece fitted luggage set was a (rare) optional extra. At least the XK120 had a boot, and a lockable one at that – many sports car owners of the time dreamed of having a boot. The XK120's boot even had a small light, which was a nice touch. The space was divided into two: the lower section housed the spare wheel and jack, while the top held a comprehensive 21-piece tool kit (in a roll-up leather wallet), the tonneau cover and a chromed rod which could hold the boot lid nearly vertical. A grease gun was also standard equipment and was stored in the engine compartment, although it was transferred to the boot on the XK140.

The XK120's second body style, the elegant Fixed-Head Coupé, was introduced in March 1951 with no detriment to the styling.

The body needs little comment since this book's illustrations vindicate the often misquoted proverb, 'A picture *can* be worth a thousand words'. It is worth noting, however, that on early cars the side lights were separate chromed affairs bolted to the top of the wings, but from late 1952 they were welded into the wings and painted. The rear light incorporated a stop light, but flashing indicators or, even, reflectors were not mandatory until 1954. Footwell flap-vents were incorporated on all models from late 1951. Under the slender, elegant front bumpers were air vents to help cool the front brakes and the lower part of the engine.

Tyres were 6.00 x 16 Dunlop Roadspeeds on 5in rims (5.5in rims were fitted from May 1952 on steel wheels only), although other types of tyre were often used for competition. Wire wheels were not available to Jaguar at a realistic price until early 1951, so pressed steel wheels, in the same colour as the body, were fitted to all early cars. In many cases such wheels might have detracted from the looks of the car – the Austin-Healey 3000 certainly lost presence when fitted with steel wheels

For some enthusiasts, William Lyons' shapely roof styling makes the Fixed-Head XK120 the prettiest car in the family. Fixed-Head interior was completely different, with plenty of wood for the dashboard and window surrounds (below) and a useful storage box behind the seats (bottom).

– but Lyons was a genius when it came to detail styling. Instead of the usual bland chromed hubcaps, there was an outer ring of chrome, a middle ring painted in the body colour and a central chromed boss with a ring motif inspired by a 'knock-off' wheel nut.

The XK120 may have been designed as a publicity stunt and intended to be only a short-run model, but nothing was skimped. Even the fuel cap, which was incorporated into a flap flush with the bodywork, had a lock. Perhaps nobody would have noticed had the fuel filler not been lockable or had the hubcaps not been so carefully styled – who discusses hubcaps when there is a 120mph car on offer? – but these are telling details. They are a tiny indicator of why the XK120 was not merely an outstanding car, but one of the few in history which deserves to be called 'great'.

Relatively few XK120s saw the home market. If they did not go Stateside they tended to sell to the Commonwealth, although some went to Europe as conditions improved there as well. When the steel-bodied car went on sale in April 1950, it had the market to itself. In America it cost about $3500 (prices varied in line with local taxes and 'port of entry') at a time when an MG TC (a pre-war design of charm but without muscle) cost $2000 and Ferraris (with performance no

better than an XK120, and rarer than hens' teeth) began at around $12,000. A Nash-Healey, which came onto the market in 1951, could be yours for about $5000, but it lagged far behind in performance and style, even when Pinin Farina was engaged to restyle it. Besides, even $5000 was a subsidised price – it is believed that each 'Farina' Nash-Healey cost $9000 to make. Nash wanted to entice punters into its showrooms and was prepared to stand a loss, a concept alien to Lyons.

Jaguar could sell every car it made, but materials were

still restricted and the capacity of the factory to make cars was limited, otherwise Jaguar might have made more than the 12,055 XK120s which did leave Coventry. Besides, in 1951 Jaguar launched the MkVII saloon, which was always intended to be the company's main model – the saloon car market is larger and more stable than the sports car market.

Regardless of how brilliant they were, Jaguar sports cars were always secondary to the saloon range, but this fact did not prevent Jaguar from introducing a Fixed-Head Coupé (FHC) version of the XK120 in March 1951 to service those markets where the weather made a Roadster a marginal choice. The styling of the pretty roof can be traced back to Lyons' styling exercise on an SS100 in 1938, and some would say that it was an even more handsome car than the Roadster.

The doors were wider and incorporated a shallow pocket on the inner panel, the steering column was adjustable for length and, of course, there were wind-up windows. The interior of the FHC was more luxurious than the Roadster's: it featured a parcel shelf and luggage box behind the seats, while walnut veneer for the dashboard and door cappings gave an air of opulence. Some of the minor controls on the dashboard were relocated, and at bottom centre was a walnut-capped ashtray. Remarkably, the FHC sold for only £10 more

From the rear, early production Fixed-Head (top) shares a family look with Jaguar's big saloons. Prototype cabin had a 'knotted' brass parcel rail behind the seats (above) – William Lyons discarded this for production after someone said it made the interior look like a hearse.

than the Roadster, which by that time cost £1078 (£1678 with purchase tax).

While the FHC was a welcome addition to the range (one became the first car in history to average more than 100mph for seven days and nights), it never sold as strongly as the Roadster, which remained easily the most

First of five Jaguar Le Mans victories, with Peter Walker and Peter Whitehead in their battle-scarred 1951 winner. The XK120C, or C-type, was based on production components.

Much later in the C-type's career, eventual winner Duncan Hamilton looks for a chance to pass Tony Rolt in the 1954 Empire Trophy at Oulton Park.

popular choice until the arrival of the XK150. In all, 7612 XK120 Roadsters were built compared with 2678 FHCs (and 1765 examples of the later Drophead Coupé).

Shortly before the 1951 Le Mans race, Jaguar unveiled the XK120C (C for 'Competition'), which quickly became known as the C-type. Its sleek body was designed by Malcolm Sayer, an ex-aircraft aerodynamicist who had the rare knack of being able to combine science with art, and who was one of the unsung heroes of the British motor industry. At a time when most cars were styled, the C-type's body was engineered.

Beneath the sleek skin was a 210bhp engine with

More XK120 Fixed-Heads were built than Dropheads because of the closed car's earlier launch, but in original right-hand drive form (right) this is the rarest version – just 194 were made. Above the radiator grille sits a proud emblem (below right).

modified cams, a lighter flywheel, bigger exhaust valves and improved porting. There was also a properly triangulated spaceframe (one of the first ever) with stressed bulkheads and channel-section steel bottom members. Front suspension was similar to the standard car and used some production components, although the torsion bars were thicker. The live rear axle was located by radius arms and an A-bracket, and was sprung on a single transverse torsion bar with hydraulic dampers. The car's dry weight of 2070lb was close to that of the less powerful, and much less competent, Aston Martin DB3.

The C-type was designed to win on the fast, smooth, Le Mans circuit and it rarely shone on twisty or bumpy tracks. After four hours in the 1951 Le Mans, the three C-types held an easy 1-2-3 but two retired with cracked oil pipes. By then no serious opposition was left in the running, so the surviving crew of Peter Whitehead and Peter Walker was able to ease off, reducing the vibration which caused the copper pipes to crack, and won by nine laps. Driving a C-type, Stirling Moss won his second TT in September, with other C-types second and fourth.

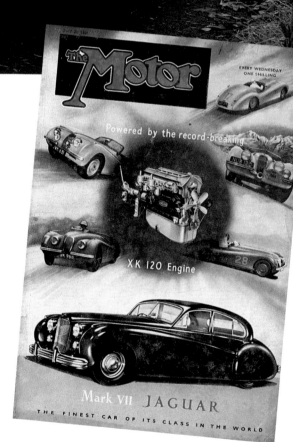

An XK120 Drophead in Suede Green (above). The focus of Jaguar's marketing was the MkVII saloon, but sports car exploits added lustre.

This cover from the 23 May 1951 issue of *The Motor* (right) is the nearest Jaguar came to directly advertising the XK120 in the UK.

Although Jaguar had eschewed direct works involvement in competition for most of its history, it entered a new phase whereby it developed and proved equipment which it then applied to both its competition and road cars. In March 1951 it offered 181bhp 'Special Equipment' (SE) versions of the XK120 as a direct result of lessons learned in racing, and some learned in the market place.

The most important difference on the SE was its more powerful engine, which developed 181bhp at 5000rpm and 203lb ft of torque at 4000rpm thanks to new camshafts, an 8:1 compression ratio, a crankshaft damper and a twin exhaust system. Less obvious improvements included stiffer springing, an optional close-ratio gear cluster, a choice of four final drive ratios,

Photographed outside the Jaguar factory, this Drophead shows off the quality fit of its folding hood.

and self-adjusting front brakes (which became standard on all models at the same time). Twin spot headlights were standard on SE models – some existing owners had taken the initiative and fitted their own. Wire wheels at last became available, in which case the spats over the rear wheels were omitted. Standard on the SE, wire wheels were specified as an option by most buyers of regular XK120s.

Buyers of the SE version could also specify individual bucket seats, which were an improvement over the previous arrangement but still not up to snuff because their backs were too flat to provide adequate lateral support. Other options included a racing windscreen and cowl, a 24-gallon fuel tank, Dunlop racing tyres, 9:1 compression ratio pistons and an even more powerful (210bhp) engine with a C-type cylinder head and 2in carburettors. In America the SE was known, unofficially, as the XK120M (M for 'Modified') while those fitted with the C-type cylinder head were known as the XK120MC (MC for 'Modified Competition').

Le Mans was the main works target for 1952, but a single car for Moss was entered in the Mille Miglia and equipped with Dunlop disc brakes. It has since been claimed that Jaguar pioneered the use of disc brakes, but this is untrue. What Jaguar did was to prove the viability and potential superiority of disc brakes which, ultimately, was of much greater value.

A form of disc brake was used by the Gulf-Miller cars at Indianapolis in 1938, but this system was based on the principles of a clutch with plates squeezing the disc. Disc brakes were seen at Indianapolis in the early post-war period, but there they were used merely to steady cars in

the corners, not for braking hard into a hairpin. It was to take a long time before discs were proven for automotive use: the 1100cc Lola Mk1 of 1958 used drums and dominated its class into the 1960s, while Porsche ran with drums in Formula 1 as late as 1961.

Disc braking was developed for aircraft because discs are more compact than drums and dissipate heat more effectively. In the early days there were different schools of thought: the Palmer system (used on the 1955 HRG 'Twin Cam' sports car) operated only on the inside of the disc. An aircraft brakes heavily only once every flight and then only for a short time, whereas cars, especially competition cars, have entirely different requirements. For a long time disc brake systems tended to be less predictable, heavier and less reliable than a good drum system. In 1949 the American Crosley 'Hot Shot' sports car became the first production model to use discs – Goodyear-Hawley 'spot' discs in the front wheels – but they were prone to seizing and were replaced by drums within a year. In 1950 some Chrysler models could be bought with four-wheel disc brakes, but they were never popular and before long Chrysler dropped them.

Jaguar worked with Dunlop and demanded a period of exclusivity for its system, which is why Aston Martin, for example, had to use drums until Girling developed a rival system. So Jaguar was not the first company to use discs, but it was the first to prove them and its involvement with Dunlop went far beyond that of a passive customer. This is Jaguar's true achievement. At Le Mans in 1955 Mercedes-Benz fitted its cars with an air brake – a rear panel which flipped up. It was widely admired at the time, but should not have been because it

Two XK120 variants. Ghia's 1954 coupé (above) exemplifies the art of the Italian coachbuilder at its best. Not quite how

Lyons envisaged the XK120, four-seater Roadster adaptation by Abbott of Farnham lacks grace (right).

was no more than a crude expedient because Mercedes-Benz, with drum brakes, could not match Jaguar's stopping distances. Do road cars today have air brakes?

In that 1952 Mille Miglia, the disc-braked C-type's debut, Moss lay fourth until he crashed with 150 miles to go, but by that time the C-type was in the usual condition of a Jaguar in a real road race – the shock absorbers had gone and the fuel tank was leaking. When he returned to England, Stirling expressed concern about the straight-line speed of the new Mercedes-Benz 300SLs and this led to a famous error...

The C-types which ran at Le Mans in 1952 retained drum brakes, but were fitted with new long-tail bodies with 'droop-snoot' nose sections to achieve a higher top speed. The aerodynamic theory was sound, but the engines overheated because of the revised plumbing to the repositioned header tank. Hasty modifications were made but the three team cars retired in the first four hours. The irony is that Mercedes-Benz paced its cars to achieve a finish and C-types with the standard body could have walked the race.

The following year, 1953, saw the introduction of the XK120 Drophead Coupé (DHC), which in essence was a Roadster with wind-up windows, quarterlights and a permanently-attached hood that sat proud of the cockpit when folded down. Coming late in the XK120's production life, the DHC is the rarest of the three body styles. It is sad to record that some DHCs which went abroad were fitted with white steering wheels.

The C-type was also offered in 1953 in 'production' form at £1495 plus tax and 43 were made, bringing the total to 53 when the 10 'racers' are included. This was

the ultimate road car since regulations insisted that cars must be road-legal, have doors and carry such items as a spare wheel and a (rudimentary) hood.

A C-type with a special body achieved 178.3mph at Jabbeke in 1953 and this became known as the C/D-type since its body was the clear ancestor to the D-type.

The first three World Champions – Giuseppe Farina, Juan-Manuel Fangio and Alberto Ascari – all bought C-types for road use. Since each, surely, could have swung a deal with Ferrari, their purchase must signify something. There is a legend that Farina bought his to be able to share the secret of Jaguar's disc brakes with Ferrari, but this is nonsense since all production C-types were fitted with drum brakes and it is unlikely that Farina, the only PhD to win a grand prix, could be so naive. This myth anyway does not explain why a car was bought by Ascari, who was Ferrari's number one driver. Besides, Ferrari was conservative to a fault and not until 1958, five years after Jaguar had proved the superiority of discs at Le Mans, would a Ferrari race with disc brakes.

Jaguar returned to Le Mans in 1953 in good order, having tested extensively. The works cars were lighter and, with triple twin-choke Weber carburettors, were even more powerful with 220bhp. The vulnerable rear end had been strengthened and twin trailing arms and a Panhard rod replaced the old A-bracket. Most significantly, of course, the team cars were fitted with Dunlop disc brakes: although there were plenty of more powerful cars in the race, the works Jaguars out-braked them by a huge margin. All three works cars finished, in first, second (after trouble with a dirty fuel filter) and fourth places. To complete the day, a private Belgian C-

type (with drum brakes) finished a trouble-free ninth. More than just a fabulous win, Jaguar had also proved that the disc brake was the brake of the future.

Other C-type successes included a win in the Reims 12 Hour race by a works car, while private C-types took second in the Spa 24 Hours and the Nürburgring 1000 Kms. With one round remaining of the newly-inaugurated World Sports Car Championship, the Carrera Panamericana in Mexico, Jaguar headed the points table, and one should remember that 1953 saw more works teams compete in the WSCC than in any other year in its history. No fewer than 15 marques scored points and for each which did there was at least one which did not. But the WSCC was not perceived to be as important as individual races, and Lyons scratched Jaguar's single entry in the Carrera Panamericana because it would have cost £30,000 to compete. Having won Le Mans, the title meant little. Ferrari did not send a team either, but a privateer's fourth place gave Ferrari the title.

So far as the works was concerned, the C-type's career concluded at the end of 1953 because Jaguar was preparing its successor, the D-type. Such is the rate of progress that the ex-works C-types did not score any notable successes in international racing in 1954, although they continued to be strong players in national racing all over the world.

The importance of the competition models, and the reason why they are described here, was the direct

relationship they had to the development of the road cars, and this remained true until the 1960s. They also added lustre to Jaguar's reputation, which was welcome. While the XK120 was in a class of its own during the first years of its life, as time went by it became less remarkable and was perceived less as a supercar and more as an accessible production model which had to fight for its place in the market against ever stronger opposition.

Other makers saw the potential of the mass-produced sports car and by mid-1953 the popular market looked like this:

	Max speed	0-60mph	Price
Austin-Healey 100	103mph	10.3sec	$3000
Chevrolet Corvette	110mph	11.0sec	$3400
Jaguar XK120	120mph	10.0sec	$3345
MG TF	85mph	20.0sec	$2200
Nash-Healey	105mph	13.0sec	$6200
Porsche 356 'Super'	95mph	12.5sec	$4200
Triumph TR2	103mph	11.9sec	$2400

On paper, the Jaguar looked the best bet – by a country mile – but other forces were at play. Sports car owners did not necessarily want outright performance

A Drophead shows off some of the features which distinguish it from a Roadster – tailored hood, taller doors and body-colour windscreen **frame. Interior is trimmed more lavishly, but two-tier boot layout, with spare wheel below, was shared with the other models.**

and many found that the TR2 fulfilled all their requirements. Others admired the personality, quirkiness and reliability of the early VW-based Porsches and were prepared to pay more than the price of an XK120 to enjoy a more expensive car which offered less performance. Yet others appreciated the style and capability of the Austin-Healey 100, and some would argue that, by 1953, the Healey outshone the XK120 in kerbside presence. They were close in price, yet Austin-Healey sold five cars to Jaguar's three.

There was little reason to buy a Nash-Healey or the early Corvette, however, and few did. The 'Vette would become a great car, but its early life was plagued by production problems with its glass-fibre body and few thought that a two-speed automatic gearbox had a place in a sports car. It may surprise some readers that there were several other American sports car projects in the 1950s, but most of them were long-forgotten failures.

By the early 1950s the American love affair with the British sports car was running a high temperature and Jaguar was at the forefront of the friendly invasion.

PRODUCTION XKs IN COMPETITION

Racing added to the XK120's stature. Leslie Johnson won with HKV 500 (left) on the XK's competition debut, in the 1949 One Hour Production Sports Car Race at Silverstone. Bira's sister car, HKV 455 (below), suffered a puncture while leading.

Handsome is as handsome does. The XK120 looked great and went well in a straight line, but was it any good? As a sports car? To allay any doubts, Jaguar entered a team of three in the 1949 One Hour Production Sports Car Race at Silverstone. One, driven by 'B. Bira' (Birabongse Bhanudej Bhanubandh, Prince of Siam) suffered a puncture when leading, but Leslie Johnson and Peter Walker brought the others home to score a decisive 1–2. XK120s won the race the following two years as well.

Five special development cars were supplied to selected drivers in 1950. Jaguar had previously avoided direct participation in racing, but this limited exercise was to lead to a serious programme which was to benefit the production cars. A sixth works-prepared car, NUB 120, was rallied by Ian Appleyard (William Lyons' son-in-law), who in 1950 won the first of a record five successive *Coupes des Alpes*, all in Jaguars.

The six special cars were officially private entries, a tactic which allowed Jaguar to distance itself from any failure while reaping the benefit of any success. This was to be a long-term policy. Although works cars were run

Jaguar's first visit to the Le Mans 24 Hours came with three XK120s in 1950. Two of the cars **lasted the race, this one of Peter Clark/Nick Haines the higher finisher in 12th place.**

The two Jaguar entries for the 1951 Mille Miglia. Stirling Moss drove HKV 500 with Frank Rainbow, **and Leslie Johnson was partnered by John Lea in JWK 651. Both retired with brake problems.**

between 1951-56, their competition programme was fairly limited. On the other hand, successful privateers were given works assistance and this policy continued until the Lightweight E-types of the 1960s.

In 1950 Clemente Biondetti, the only four-times winner of the Mille Miglia, briefly led the combined Tour of Sicily and Targa Florio in his XK120, but he retired with a broken con-rod. A disappointment, but a useful lesson and thereafter all con-rods were crack-tested at the factory. Four of the five 'racers' ran in the Mille Miglia, and Leslie Johnson brought his home fifth, with Biondetti eighth despite a broken rear spring. For a production sports car to finish fifth was a commendable effort (no British car of any description was ever to finish higher), but the race highlighted the car's faults, which included inadequate brakes.

Three XK120s went to Le Mans as a recce in 1950: Lyons knew the publicity value of a race which, uniquely, emphasised the car rather than its drivers. His growing interest in motor racing, however, was solely as a marketing tool, since he had no passion for it. Jaguars raced only when there was a potential profit, which

explains why the works team never completed a full season of World Sports Car Championship events. Leslie Johnson and Bert Hadley ran as high as second at half-distance in the 1950 Le Mans, but having to supplement their brakes by slowing down with the gearbox caused the clutch centre to pull out in the 22nd hour. The other two cars finished 12th and 15th. Again, the exercise had shown a flaw, and the Bergalite driven clutch of the first cars was replaced by a clutch with solid plates.

Tommy Wisdom, a journalist who was also a gifted driver and a recipient of one of the special cars, believed in the potential of a 20-year-old youngster called Stirling Moss, who had been refused a car by Jaguar on the grounds that he lacked experience. Wisdom entered Moss in the 1950 Tourist Trophy at Dundrod, which was run in a downpour. But Moss, being Moss, regarded that as his advantage since it made life easier for the brakes. Stirling duly took the first of what was to be seven victories in the Tourist Trophy, with Peter Whitehead second, on the road and on handicap, in another XK120. This success confirmed Jaguar's intention to go racing seriously. After the race Moss was

Famous XK120 racer. JWK 977 was driven regularly – in more standard form than seen here – by Peter Walker in 1950 and also ran at Le Mans that year.

signed by Lyons to lead the works team that Jaguar proposed to run, and the next day he turned 21 – it was an important landmark in his career.

Since Stirling won more races, in more types of car, than any top-class driver in history, his comments in his book *My Cars, My Career* (co-written with Doug Nye) about racing an XK120 are important: "It had quite soft, long-travel suspension, a lot of smooth power for the time and although people have since criticised its gearbox, steering and brakes, believe me, they were all good enough by the standards of the time!

"Despite its considerable weight, the XK120 never handled heavily. You had to show it who was master sometimes as it tended to lift its inside rear wheel and wag its tail under power, but it was – and remains – a particularly important car for me...a car which I recall with admiration, and gratitude."

In November 1950, at Pebble Beach, Phil Hill gave Jaguar its first important American victory in an XK120 which he and Richie Ginther, perhaps the most gifted driver-engineer of the time, had modified. They lightened the car, bored out the engine to 3.8 litres, and fitted Alfin brake drums and Borrani wire wheels to help cool the brakes – later they admitted that perhaps they

The imperturbable Stirling Moss on his way to winning the Production Sports Car Race at Silverstone's *Daily Express* International Trophy meeting in 1951.

had also made the car a little nose-heavy. Still, Hill won and before long some of the six quasi-works cars, and some serious privateers, also had wire wheels.

Winning the One Hour Production Car Race at Silverstone in 1949 was trumpeted, but the XK120 was a brand-new design up against cars which, at best, had pre-war engines in post-war chassis. The XK120 had failed where it mattered most, in the Mille Miglia and at Le Mans. Jaguar decided that in future it would build

Famous XK120 rally car. NUB 120 gave Ian and Pat Appleyard the first ever *Coupe d'Or*, for three successive Alpine Rallies without penalties.

The Appleyards in a much-published but classic pose on the 1950 Alpine (left), and on the way to third place in the 1952 RAC Rally (above).

More rallying XK120s. On the 1952 Scottish Rally, G.P.Denham misjudges a downhill braking test at the famous Rest-And-Be-Thankful Hill (left). Not quite as famous as NUB 120, but RJH 400 had a good 1954 season for Eric Haddon and Charles Vivian, finishing first in class on the Alpine (below).

bespoke cars for racing – and it began with the C-type (or XK120C) in 1951. In the meantime the XK120 served plenty of competition drivers very well.

Ian and Pat (*née* Lyons) Appleyard won the first-ever *Coupe d'Or* for completing three successive Alpine Rallies without incurring a single penalty point. This was virtually a race held in stages over the Alps when the roads were largely unmetalled and Armco had not been invented. It was an amazing achievement and a generation of schoolboys insisted on having NUB 120 as the number plate on any model XK120 they owned.

Johnny Claes (a Belgian jazz band leader and Grand Prix driver) and Jacques Ickx (father of Jacky) won the 1951 Liège-Rome-Liège Rally in a XK120 – the first time a British car had won an event that was even tougher than the Alpine. Again, this was virtually a race run in stages.

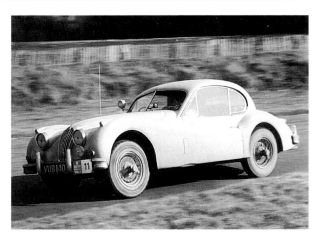

The XK140 had far less competition success, but Ian and Pat Appleyard did manage to finish second on the 1956 RAC Rally in a Fixed-Head.

XKs raced all over the world. Two XK120s with unknown drivers lead away an SCCA field at **Sebring in 1954 (above), while Jorge Caamano spins out of a 1951 race in Buenos Aires (right).**

Among other rally successes were a 1-2-3 in the 1951 French Rallye Soleil, and wins in the 1951 Tour de France, the Morecombe Rally, the RAC Rally in 1951 and 1953, and the 1953 Acropolis. The Morecombe Rally does not sound terribly exciting today, but a glance down the entry list would prove otherwise. Rallying then was not the specialised category it is today, and most of the top drivers from all branches of the sport took part.

When it came to racing, the XK120 was most at home in club events for production cars, a category which became increasingly important on both sides of the Atlantic in the 1950s. The XK120 was outstandingly competitive in this area: simply nothing in the over 3000cc class could compare with it for years, save when race organisers took a very flexible view of what was a 'production car'.

This flexibility also benefited Jaguar because the successes of the initial batch of lightweights were included along with the steel-bodied mass-produced cars. In fact, the aluminium-bodied cars did most of the winning, and Jaguar's Competition Department gave special help to some drivers. It was, however, the very first steel-bodied car (JWK 675) which won the 1951 One Hour Production Sports Car Race at Silverstone. Of course, it helped that it was driven by Stirling Moss and that its engine produced 196bhp...

Here is not the place to dwell on this area of competition. Jaguar fried bigger fish than club racing and there were so many successes at club level that one could

not begin to chronicle them. Besides, the combination of the batch of 'lightweights' and discreet works involvement makes objective assessment very difficult.

Take, for example, the 'Ancient Egyptian', which was run successfully by 'Dick' Protheroe. It acquired its nickname because Protheroe had bought it while serving with the RAF in Egypt (he claimed that he found it by the pyramids), and it was one of the original batch of lightweights. Protheroe was a very competent driver who, with works help, developed his car to the limit, so it finished up with a C-type head, D-type camshafts, off-set wire wheels, disc brakes and greatly modified suspension. It was a works-assisted XK120 Special rather than an XK120, but it counted as a production car and Protheroe enjoyed great success with it.

Because the XK120's engine and shape were so fundamentally competent, many people were able to produce what were effectively specials with the overall shape of the original. In Britain John Pearson, a noted Jaguar expert, starred in club racing 25 years after the XK120's debut until his glassfibre-bodied special was outlawed in 1973. In America, Bob Smiley was winning races much later than 1973 in his XK120 Special. Also in America, XK120s and XK140s were sometimes fitted with domestic V8 engines in the late 1950s and early 1960s. Some owners enjoyed a measure of success with these cars, which sometimes had well over 250bhp on tap, but the rear suspension had to be modified to avoid axle tramp and limited slip differentials were needed.

The first landmark in Jaguar's record-breaking efforts. Ron 'Soapy' Sutton about to make his famous 132.6mph run along the Jabbeke autoroute in Belgium on 30 May 1949.

The later models, the XK140 and XK150, put on weight and were no longer as far ahead of the opposition as the original. It was still possible, however, for a near-standard privately-entered XK140 coupé (with 25,000 miles on the clock) to hold 14th place at Le Mans in 1956 until the 21st hour, when it was disqualified for re-fuelling a lap too early.

Although the XK140 won no major events, Chuck Wallace won the SCCA C Production Championship in 1955. Ian Appleyard was second in the 1956 RAC Rally and in the Mille Miglia that year an XK140 driven by a Frenchman named Guyot won the 'Price Category', which was a class for mass-produced sports cars. In 1959-60, David Hobbs had a string of successes in British club racing in in a coupé fitted with a 'Mechamatic' (automatic) gearbox designed by his father.

Even these comparatively slight achievements were more than the XK150 managed. Walt Hansgen won a couple of races in America with an XK150S, and another car won its class in the 1960 Tulip Rally. An unmodified XK150S won British three club races in 1959 driven by Don Parker: this was Don's road car and he was in his 50s, but one has to note that Don Parker remains, with 126 victories, the most successful Formula 3 driver in history. Assessing a car's significance in club racing is an historian's minefield...

While we are at it, the putative 14th place by an

Another Jabbeke record run, this time on 21 October 1953. Norman Dewis reached an incredible 172.4mph in this bubble-topped XK120, and Jaguar shouted the message in American magazines.

XK140 at Le Mans came in 1956, when, following the tragedy previous year, sports racers were limited to 2.5 litres and a 750cc DB-Panhard finished tenth. As Benjamin Disraeli said, "There are lies, damned lies, and statistics".

The true importance of the XKs in competition is four-fold. It was an XK120 which caused a major manufacturer to recognise the genius of Stirling Moss. The XK played an important part in the development of American sports car racing, which nurtured the careers of many superb drivers. It was an outstanding rally car – the

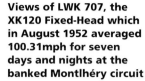

Views of LWK 707, the XK120 Fixed-Head which in August 1952 averaged 100.31mph for seven days and nights at the banked Montlhéry circuit near Paris. The four drivers, looking relaxed before the test , are, from left, Jack Fairman, Stirling Moss, Bert Hadley and Leslie Johnson.

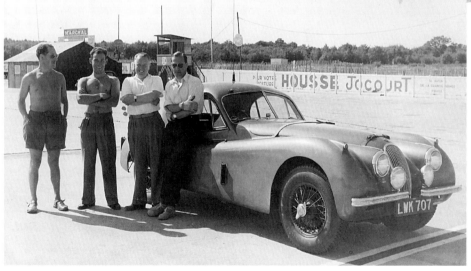

Alpine and the Liège-Rome-Liège were mighty events. And finally, it broke records.

Late in 1950 an XK120 was taken to the banked Montlhéry track near Paris and ran for 24 hours at over 107mph, an unprecedented feat and one of many 'firsts' for the model. It is not a direct comparison, but it is worth noting that the average speed of the winner at Le Mans that year was under 90mph and the lap record there was just over 102mph. The following year a modified XK120 was taken to Jabbeke and achieved 172mph, the highest speed ever attained by a sports car. It was even faster than the Mercedes–Benz 300SLR on

the Mulsanne Straight at Le Mans in 1955. Also in 1951 an XK120 was taken to Montlhéry and covered 131.83 miles in an hour.

These extraordinary records added to the legend of the XK120 in a way it is difficult to comprehend today. Twenty-four hours at 107mph was a glimpse of the future for all motorists, and caught the imagination in a way which is virtually impossible for a car to do today unless it is something like the McLaren F1 – about which you can only dream unless you have a disposable income of at least £1 million a year.

In 1952 a specially prepared, but basically standard, XK120 Fixed-Head Coupé went to Montlhéry and averaged 100.31mph for seven days and nights. It was not just the speed that was impressive, but also the reliability under far from ideal conditions, since the days were hot, the nights were cold, and the capacity of the batteries would not permit additional lights. The car covered 16,851.71 miles during the week and the run was so uneventful that the drivers had to invent practical jokes to keep their interest alive.

This, surely, is what real record-breaking is about, not strapping a jet engine to four wheels to propel some punter over a measured mile. It was real life and for the

ordinary customer with his Morris, Fiat, Renault or Ford it provided a tantalising glimpse of what motoring in the future might be like. The greatness of the XK120 is that it promised a new era when it sat on its stand at the 1948 London Motor Show and it delivered more than the most optimistic observer could have dreamed of.

THE XK140

In late 1954 Jaguar announced the XK140, but anyone thinking the new designation indicated a car capable of 140mph was in for a disappointment because this was merely a model number. It would have been more logical had the car been called the XK130, and it has been said that nobody at the factory can remember why it was not. But XK130 does evoke the number 13, and while no senior people at the factory are known to have been superstitious (touch wood!), it was thought that '140' had a better ring.

An original right-hand drive XK140 Roadster is the rarest XK model of all with just 49 sold in the UK, but this version was popular in the US.

The XK140 was essentially a consolidation of the best aspects of the XK120 and incorporated some features previously available only as optional extras. It also addressed some of the shortcomings of the earlier cars but was already beginning to look dated, although it was an all-round improvement over the XK120.

Most cars were still being exported into the XK140 period – here a shipment of Roadsters waits to be loaded on a misty winter morning at Dagenham Dock.

The XK120 had exerted considerable influence on the way 1950s sports cars were designed, but some of its main styling cues had quickly been discarded. Cars which followed it did not have vertical radiator grilles, for example, and the headlights were set at the front of the wing line. The wing lines themselves had become softer and bonnets had become less prominent.

A new cast radiator grille, with seven slats to the XK120's 12 and with the Jaguar badge incorporated at the top, was not only cheaper to make but also helped the car's cooling in slow-moving traffic. Apart from the grille, the main identifying feature was the use at front and rear of heavier new bumpers with overriders. While few thought these an aesthetic improvement, they were unquestionably a practical one. Philip Porter, an authority on Jaguars, records that an XK140 in Edinburgh was once rammed in the back by a bus – the car was undamaged but the front of the bus was stoved in.

A chrome strip ran from the top of the new grille to the division between the two halves of the windscreen. Another chrome strip running down the boot lid was interrupted by a badge recording Jaguar's wins at Le Mans – this became a sure way of telling a car's age since Jaguar won in 1955, 1956 and 1957. The boot lid itself was 6in shorter than on the XK120, and the rear number plate was attached to the lower body panel, between the

twin rear bumpers, rather than being on the lid itself.

The headlights were more powerful, and a popular option was the twin spotlights which continued as standard on the SE model. A new rear light cluster incorporated a reflector, but flashing indicators were fitted only at the front and were operated by a switch on top of the dashboard. Pressed steel wheels remained the standard fitting, but the hubcaps were completely chromed and chromed rim trims were an option – but most buyers specified the wire wheels that were standard on SE models.

Since we are talking about the mid-1950s, the wire wheels were sometimes chromed, although Heaven alone knows why. Wire wheels with uncracked chrome spokes indicate that a car has been used for cruising only, and has not been driven as it deserves to be. It was more usual for the wheels to be painted silver, or the colour of the body, while having chromed locking nuts.

Ivory white steering wheels were sometimes fitted to export models and whitewall tyres were an increasingly popular option. A rear-view mirror mounted on the centre of the scuttle was standard, but many owners fitted wing mirrors and other accessories which were coming onto the market. A 'button' handbrake replaced the 'fly-off' type – another detail which tells how Jaguar had changed its own perception of the model – but customers

Tail view shows some of the XK140's detail differences: bumper, tail lights, boot lid and brightwork were all new. Ignoring the non-standard steering wheel, grab handle and Halda Tripmaster, the interior was little changed. Engine power increased to 190bhp or 210bhp in Special Equipment form, with the optional C-type head fitted here giving even more.

Stylish brochure renderings of Drophead and Fixed-Head XK140s, published in 1956.

disliked this and the 'fly-off' handbrake was revived in September 1956.

As a concession to the American market, a Borg-Warner three-speed automatic transmission was offered as an option in October 1956, late in the XK140's life. Fewer than 400 buyers took the opportunity, but it indicates a changing view of the car's character, not least by its maker. Other options included windscreen washers, a C-type cylinder head and a Laycock de Normanville overdrive operating on the top three gears.

In order to create more cockpit space, the engine, scuttle and windscreen were all moved 3in forward – which meant that few panels were common with the XK120 – and the doors were lengthened to compensate. The occupants received redesigned footwells, giving more legroom (but the DHC had longer footwells than

other models). The driving position improved partly because of this extra footwell space (and better seat adjustment), but also because a universal joint in the steering column allowed the wheel to be angled. Moving the engine might upset the dynamic balance and styling of some cars, but the overall lines of the XK140 were unaffected and the car's handling actually improved.

The roofline was raised by 1.5in on the Fixed-Head Coupé and extended a further 6.5in to the rear to give considerably more cockpit space, with little injury to its looks, and enlarging the rear window was an aesthetic as well as a practical improvement. The FHC had an interior light operated by a manual switch.

Both the DHC and FHC had modified rear bulkheads to permit the fitting of small 'plus two' rear seats. For most practical purposes these provided extra luggage accommodation, although children could be carried for short distances. A typical Jaguar touch was that the padded back panels on the occasional seats could be

Prototype XK140 Roadster photographed at the factory with a makeshift 'studio' backdrop – in other words two blokes holding up a sheet. This shot was taken well before launch because those are XK120 bodyshells stacked in the background.

detached and used as a cushion by an adult sitting across the car. In order to accommodate the extra seats, the previous twin six-volt batteries were replaced on the DHC by a single 12-volt battery behind the left-hand front wheel, although on the FHC the six-volt batteries were retained but moved to new positions, in a box in each front wing.

Another improvement from the driver's point of view was the replacement of the old Burman recirculating ball steering with an Alford & Alder rack and pinion system. It made the steering much lighter and permitted the use of a smaller steering wheel, which had a flat horn button. The often-criticised brakes were also upgraded (wire wheels anyway improved cooling and lessened the risk of brake-fade), the thicker torsion bars from the XK120 SE were fitted, and Girling telescopic dampers replaced the old lever-arm system – many small changes added up to a significant dynamic improvement.

The chassis remained similar to the original concept, but was altered in detail to take the new front bumpers and rear dampers. On the Roadster the front bulkhead was raised by 1in. Doors continued to be skinned in aluminium until October 1956, when steel skinning was adopted for the DHC and FHC.

Compared with the XK120, the XK140 put on about 200lb for each of the three variants – but in all cases the extra weight was in part offset by the use of a more powerful engine. The compression ratio was raised to 8:1 since better quality fuel was becoming widely available, steel main bearing caps replaced the previous iron caps,

and the engine delivered 190bhp at 5500rpm with 210lb ft torque at 2500rpm. This power improvement meant that the performance of the XK140 remained broadly in line with the XK120, while the increase in torque, which was lower in the rev range, made it more lively in serious cross-country driving.

Once again a Special Equipment model was offered, and this produced 210bhp at 5750rpm and 213lb ft torque at 4000rpm. As usual the SE was more than an engine package and items such as twin spotlights, close-ratio gears, wire wheels and overdrive were standard. Other performance accessories, such as the C-type head and 9:1 compression ratio pistons, remained options, but a buyer living in a country where good quality fuel was not available could go the other way and specify a 7:1 compression ratio.

Road testers still did not exactly coincide with their findings. One test of an FHC SE version recorded a top speed of 129.25mph and covered the 0-60mph sprint in 11sec. Another, of a Roadster, returned 121mph and 0-60mph in 8.4sec. The FHC was about 100lb heavier and slightly more efficient aerodynamically, but this does not explain the discrepancies. There were, in fact, so many options of tune and final drive ratio that there is no such thing as a standard set of performance figures for an XK140.

By the time the XK140 appeared, the sports car market had changed dramatically. For a start, the Jaguar was no longer the world's ultimate sports car, the Mercedes-Benz 300SL 'gullwing' now holding that

position with no serious opposition. It cost more than twice as much as a Jaguar, certainly, and it was made in much smaller numbers, but it did hold the number one spot. The wonder is not that the 300SL had overtaken Jaguar, but that a relatively inexpensive mass-produced car could have been the ultimate fantasy of sports car drivers for so long.

Many of the firms that had been rivals in the market in 1948 had vanished or were on their last legs. In Britain production had all but ceased of cars such as Allard, Dellow, Frazer Nash, Healey (not Austin-Healey), HRG and Lea-Francis. They had flourished until a relaxation of government regulations in Britain had changed a sellers' market into a buyers' market and then, lacking new models or ideas, they had foundered.

Aston Martin was strong, by its terms, but the DB2/4 cost nearly twice as much as an XK140 and, although beautifully styled and built, offered less performance. AC had introduced the Ace, but this again was for a niche market, and it was not until the Ace received the Bristol engine did it become a truly desirable car. Sunbeam Talbot had limited success with the Alpine which had little to commend it at the price – in Britain it cost £1212 to the £1598 of the XK140 Roadster and would barely top 90mph. The Swallow Doretti, at £1101, found its place in the market, but was killed by the ultimatum which Lyons delivered to Swallow's parent company. The antiquated Singer Roadster (£737) was still in production, in theory, but was laid to rest in 1955.

The Austin-Healey 100 (£1063) and Triumph TR2

(£886) opened up new markets, but MG was still stuck with the TF (£780) because internal politics within BMC delayed the introduction of the MGA in case it should take market share from Austin-Healey. Heaven alone knows how many sales that cost BMC, but Jaguar was outside such destructive politicking, although

eventually it was to become sucked into the morass of the British Leyland Motor Corporation. But this lay well into the future. One of the pleasant things about writing on the XK-series is that it is a story of a great company making great cars which enjoyed continuous success.

Most of the great French makers were fading fast or had already closed their doors. In 1950 the French government introduced a new package of welfare and pensions and, to pay for it, had imposed a levy on employers of 48 per cent of their employees' wages. This encouraged mass-production and killed the labour-intensive luxury car makers and the parallel French coachbuilding industry. Two great traditions died in the spiritual home of the sports car.

In Italy Alfa Romeo, only the second company to mass-produce a double overhead camshaft engine, grew ever stronger. While it is unlikely that Alfa took many sales from Jaguar, it expanded the GT market. Ferrari and Maserati each made nominal GT cars, but really they were just slightly civilised sports racers. Fiat made small numbers of the 8V and several tiny Italian firms such as Siata, Moretti and Stanguellini found small spaces in the American market.

The difference is hard to spot at a glance, but the XK140 Fixed-Head's roofline is 1.5in higher and 6.5in longer than an XK120's.

Porsche grew ever stronger with the 356 (£1786-£1956), BMW made a small number of V8-engined sports and GT cars, and Mercedes-Benz had the 300SL (£4392), which sold mainly in America but added a shine to the company's reputation in all markets. Nash-Healey gave up the struggle in 1954 and the Chevrolet Corvette seemed destined to follow it until Ford introduced the Thunderbird – phew! We had a narrow escape there.

Jaguar held its own, even if the XK140 could not quite replicate the excitement of its elder sister. At a time when manufacturers often completely re-styled their cars every two or three years, with annual face-lifts in between, some were disappointed that Jaguar had been so conservative. Part of the reason was that Lyons had decided the future lay with strong designs which received constant improvement, but the factory was also at full-stretch preparing the 2.4-litre saloon, the company's first car with unitary construction, for launch in 1956.

The XK140 received a new cast grille, which was cheaper to make than the XK120's (right). Inside a Fixed-Head there were only detail changes in the front (below), but tiny 'plus two' seats appeared in the back (below right).

Another factor was that Lyons was in touch with his market in a way which few company bosses can equal. He knew the limits of his factory's capacity, and knew that he could maintain sales of his sports cars at a steady rate even though this would mean a reduction in Jaguar's share of an expanding market. With the tooling costs ameliorated, Jaguar could continue to offer amazing value while increasing profits. It is hard to think of any other

company founder who has shown such flair in the market, let alone one whose personal contribution to his product has been so great.

Although Jaguar never embraced competition as an end in itself, Lyons was very aware of the status which success in motor sport, particularly at Le Mans, had given his company. He never sanctioned a full-blown attempt on the World Sports Car Championship, but

concentrated only on events which might show a commercial return. No works Jaguars appeared in the Mille Miglia after 1953, no works Jaguars ever ran in the Buenos Aires 1000 Kms (the traditional opening round of the WSCC), and only occasionally did they appear at circuits such as the Nürburgring. Often the works team missed WSCC races to turn out at comparatively minor events such as support races for the International Trophy at Silverstone, but these events were often televised.

On the other hand Lyons was acutely aware of the value of competition in testing new technology. Jaguar's development of the modern disc brake, hand-in-glove with Dunlop, is a contribution whose importance cannot be under-estimated. Jaguar also experimented with Lucas fuel injection long before it was fitted to any road car, and its experience in competition with this system kept the company wary of fuel injection for a long time. It was the right decision as Triumph discovered to its cost: the mechanical Lucas system was not the epitome of reliability.

Competition cars were fine, but Lyons, the hard-headed Lancashire businessman, made sure they paid their way, or at least a good part of their way. A new design could be sanctioned for use by the works, but it was then offered to customers so that the cost could be absorbed. This was the policy which made the immortal C-type and D-type into production cars, and allowed some lucky owners to drive a Le Mans winner on the road.

Jaguar unveiled the D-type in April 1954 in time for Le Mans in June. Just as Malcolm Sayer had managed to

Jaguar went racing to 'improve the breed' – to bring technical and publicity benefits that would sell more road cars. This is Norman Dewis at MIRA testing a short-nose D-type, with tufts of wool attached to examine air flow.

combine style with aerodynamic efficiency with the C-type, so he made a quantum leap with the D-type. It was a compact car with a wheelbase of just 7ft 6in and a scuttle height of only 31in, and at 1900lb it was significantly lighter than the C-type.

The central section, made from magnesium alloy, was a monocoque structure surrounding a tubular frame which ran forward from just behind the seats to the front of the car. Rear suspension was by a live rear axle and twin radius arms with a transverse torsion bar and an A-bracket, while the longitudinal torsion bar and double wishbone front suspension from earlier cars was retained. Detail attention to the dry-sumped engine paid off with increased power, initially 245bhp, and the engine was canted forwards eight degrees to reduce bonnet height. Disc brakes and aluminium alloy Dunlop wheels with knock-off hubcaps were standard.

Works D-types made their debut at Le Mans in 1954 and proved to be very quick in a straight line. One was timed on the Mulsanne Straight at 173mph, nearly 15mph quicker than the 4.9-litre Ferraris which had about 100bhp more. The final stages of the race were thrilling, with a battle in pouring rain between one surviving Ferrari (whose drum brakes were cooled by the rain) and one D-type. The Ferrari won by 2.2 miles (a little over a minute) on the road, but everyone agreed that it had been a sensational debut for the D-type and shortly afterwards it took its first race victory, in the Reims 12 Hours.

Later in 1954 Jaguar listed the D-type as a production car at an ex-tax price of £1895. To put that into perspective, it was less than five times the price of a 948cc Standard Ten saloon, whose equivalent today is something like the Ford Fiesta. A Le Mans winner for five Fiestas?

On production D-types the magnesium alloy of the original monocoque was replaced by a non-stressed aluminium tub to keep the price down and make repairs easier. It can be argued that it was the first car in the world to be offered with an efficient disc brake system on all four wheels. As the D-type was launched as a production car at the 1954 London Motor Show, so Austin-Healey announced the 100S, also with four-wheel disc brakes. The Healey was more closely related to a production car than the D-type, and had first raced earlier, but Jaguar sold 50 examples (then the definition of a production car) before the Healey.

For 1955 the works D-types had longer noses, and a new cylinder head which increased power to 285bhp, but it was a privately owned car which scored the model's first WSCC victory when one entered by Briggs Cunningham won the Sebring 12 Hours. Jaguar's main effort was, as always, Le Mans, and there it won. It was not a joyous victory since this was the year of the accident which cost the lives of over 80 spectators, and Mercedes-Benz withdrew its team when comfortably in the lead. No win at Le Mans is ever inconsiderable, but this one had a hollow ring to it.

During the 1955 season private D-types took numerous wins and places in lesser races and, since they were road-legal and utterly reliable, they were often driven to the circuits. Jaguar also experimented with a de Dion rear axle on a D-type, which was another instance of the company using competition to essay its thoughts on future production car. And as we will see, Jaguar's final appearance with an XK-engined works car in a major race proved the independent rear suspension system which was to feature on the E-type and numerous saloon models.

So far as William Lyons was concerned, motor racing was a tool for his company to use to its best advantage – only incidentally was it a sport. Motor sport was like tearing up ten pound notes and setting fire to the pieces, but Lyons wanted a return and he was right. If motor racing has any value to a manufacturer, it is not to feed

Two D-types racing in anger. At Goodwood in 1955 Duncan Hamilton drifts through Fordwater in chassis XKD 406 (top), while at Le Mans in 1956

Ron Flockhart takes the chequered flag in chassis XKD 501 for the second of three consecutive D-type wins in the French classic (above).

the fantasies of a few executives, but to improve the breed and to increase sales. Lyons was perhaps the first magnate to achieve the right balance in his company's motor sport programme.

There is a story, perhaps apocryphal, that a potential customer once approached David Brown, who then owned Aston Martin, and suggested that he was prepared

XK140 in Drophead form, this one painted Maroon with Biscuit hood and interior: on all models the engine, scuttle and windscreen were moved forward by 3in to give more cockpit room.

to buy a car but it had to be 'at cost'. Brown informed him that 'at cost' meant he would pay £1000 over list price. Lyons most definitely was not a multi-millionaire indulging a fancy.

Another win was achieved at Le Mans in 1956, but with a car entered by Ecurie Ecosse – two of the works cars were eliminated in a multiple crash while the third had problems with its Lucas fuel injection. The significance of the win in the context of a book about the XK series is that, following the 1955 tragedy, prototypes were restricted to 2.5 litres and only production cars were permitted unlimited engines. Aston Martin was able to convince the organisers that its 3-litre DB3S had sold 50 examples (it had not) whereas Jaguar really had sold 50 D-types and so its victory was kosher.

This race convinced Lyons that there was no point in running a works team if a private team could beat the factory, and at the end of 1956 Jaguar retired from active racing. The team cars were sold to Ecurie Ecosse and with them went works assistance. It was, in essence, a

return to the situation of 1949-50, when some favoured customers were permitted to run 'private entries' with Jaguar's assistance.

While Lyons remained in control of Jaguar no other official works team appeared, although some 'Lightweight' E-types were virtually works cars. Lyons did sanction the fabulous XJ13, however, and this was a spit away from a full competition programme when the company became embroiled in the British Leyland Motor Corporation.

Meanwhile, back at the farm, the XK140 was an improvement over the XK120 in every way save perhaps aesthetically – the slim front bumpers and delicate radiator grille on the XK120 had been exquisite. Few stayed at home, however, and America continued to take most of the annual production of approximately 3000 sports cars. Only 73 examples of the Roadster, the most popular variant, were made with right-hand drive, for example, and only 47 stayed at home with the rest exported to some of the 50 or so countries, including Australia and South Africa, which drive on the left.

Jaguar's 3000 a year compares with an annual production of about 5000 examples of the Austin-Healey 100 and its derivatives. Jaguar and Healey each had a fairly secure niche in the market, but it would be the

Like the Fixed-Head, the Drophead had a modified rear bulkhead to allow two small seats to be installed in the back. Tail badge records Jaguar's Le Mans successes – later XK140s would also boast of victories in 1955 and 1956.

cheaper sports cars that would expand the sports car market. Although sports cars accounted for less than 20 per cent of Jaguar's production, they were the company's main product in the USA. It would be some time before Jaguar saloons became popular there.

Despite the European perception of Jaguar as a maker of high quality cars with outstanding performance for the price, not all American buyers, even those who were besotted by the XK, were unstinting in their praise of the car's reliability. Among them there circulated the wry joke that to run one you had to buy two – that way you would have one in your drive while the other was being repaired. Here we are dealing with a specific perspective: in the 1950s Americans expected even the most humble domestic model to cover over 100,000 miles without drama. America could mass-produce cars up to a standard, and down to a price, with an efficiency that nobody else could dream of. The engineering was not sophisticated, but it worked.

If Europeans sneered that American cars could go as fast as they did simply because they had massive engines, so be it. The fact remains that they were quick, and you could probably have air conditioning as well. The European automotive industry was unable to match the standards of production and reliability which Americans

An XK140 with a difference. This striking car, based on a Special Equipment XK140 chassis, was built in 1955 by Italian coachbuilder Boano of Turin and designed by Raymond Loewy for his own use.

took for granted and non-Americans had different expectations of a motor car.

Then again, it may be a case that the relatively few Jaguar dealers felt they were able to charge a premium when carrying out, say, a routine service, and that the more complicated the work, the greater the premium. Few American Jaguar dealers handled the marque exclusively and the mechanic who had to re-fit a soft-top, for example, may have been starting from scratch. It has also been suggested that the American importer priced spare parts according to what it felt the market would bear rather than what an individual component cost to make. Taking all these elements together, it is not surprising that Jaguar's image was not perfect.

Some modern American critics have suggested that Jaguars were great designs and, when they were running, they were great bargains, but they were made carelessly. In fact, a fairer assessment of Jaguars in the 1950s might be that the quality and reliability of bought-in components were not all they might have been. Not for nothing ran the quip, 'Joseph Lucas – Prince of Darkness'. One of the principal ways in which John Egan was able to transform Jaguar's standards in the late 1970s and early 1980s was to get tough with suppliers.

At least Jaguar was not subjected to the same indignity as Maserati and Ferrari in the 1960s when firms were established to re-wire new cars. They called it 'taking out the spaghetti'. When Walter Matthau, playing an ageing

playboy in the movie *The New Leaf*, lurched along in his misfiring, overheating Ferrari, the joke was only possible because everyone knew that was how Ferraris behaved in traffic. There was a further subtext in a Ferrari being an appropriate car for a washed-out roué to drive. I know of no movie gags about Jaguars...

Some suppliers always lagged behind the vision of William Lyons. It was a little like a top-class director staging a production of Hamlet and, having assembled stars for the leading roles, finding that he has to take pot luck with the supporting cast. A brilliant concept may remain, but if the actor playing Osric comes on wearing Elizabethan costume and a digital watch, it can spoil the overall effect.

THE XK150

The English idyll. Happy
couple, beautiful
countryside and a Jaguar

XK150S Roadster. But the
car, strangely, is left-
hand drive...

With the XK150 came the culmination of the XK line, and for some it was a great disappointment. Many people felt that it had lost the spirit of the XK120 and the American author, Rich Taylor, has compared the XK150 with the MG TF – a warmed-over design, a stop-gap, when a clean sheet of paper was needed. It is not hard to see the point: Jaguar had not made the ultimate fantasy car for some years, and by 1957 the ultimate fantasy for most people would have been a Ferrari 250GT with a Pininfarina body.

In fact, Lyons had designed a sleek replacement body which was completely new in every way, but was vetoed on the grounds of cost. The XK140 had a separate chassis, but from 1956 new Jaguar saloons had unitary construction and it seemed clear that whatever replaced the XK140 would have a relatively short production life because a more modern chassis would soon be needed. Although to most eyes the XK150 looked completely different from an XK140, the panels were actually made using the same tooling. The bonnet, for example, was an XK140 panel with a 4in fillet.

Jaguar has set the automotive world back on its heels more often than any other marque, with the SS1, SS100, XK120, MkVII, C-type, D-type, XKSS, Mark II, E-

type, XJ6, E-type V12, and so on. It is the XK150's misfortune that it was not one of the cars which startled. It was the most competent of the XK line, no question, and it was still the best package on the sports car market, but it did not shake the world.

By 1957 the XK150's performance was no longer remarkable – the Chevrolet Corvette was cheaper and in top spec could match the Jaguar. Some felt that the XK150's softer lines were akin to a once-dazzling beauty who had filled out and put on weight – still a damned handsome woman but you should have seen her in her prime. Hardly anyone bothered to use an XK150 for competition work: the XK's days of glory in racing and rallying had more or less finished in 1951-52 when Jaguar produced the C-type.

Times had changed and the XK150 reflected that. Times have also changed since its introduction and today some people have come to regard the XK150 as the most handsome and refined of the series, and the one which is most desirable today if it is to be used frequently. It is one thing to own a car which is wheeled out once or twice a year, but another to run a classic on a daily basis. Late in the day the XK150 has become valued for what it is, a

The XK150 in Drophead form. The broad grille and fattened flanks make this model instantly distinguishable from the XK140.

superb and able car, rather than the over-weight XK120 that contemporary critics saw.

The XK evolved from being an out-and-out sports car to something more akin to a grand tourer, but GT cars were increasingly popular in the late 1950s. While Austin-Healey, Triumph and MG catered very successfully for the young blood who wanted a sports car to pull the girls, Jaguar was moving towards the buyer who had made his way in life and wanted to recapture some of the joys of youth without sacrificing every creature comfort.

When the XK120 came out, it was the only sports car to have if you could afford one. By 1957 Jaguar aimed at a specific section of the market against increasing competition, and it succeeded in maintaining its output of sports cars at around 3000 a year. Triumph would shift about 20,000 TR3As a year in the late 1950s, but it also became too dependent on its sports car range. Sports cars tend to sell best when the economy is booming, and sales

Tail view shows another angle on the XK150's style modernisation – there are new tail lamps and a square number plate housing. The Drophead interior is different, too, with a new instrument layout and walnut now absent. The tail badge still keeps up to date with Le Mans victories, but this early Drophead was built before the last of Jaguar's five successes at the Sarthe.

slump when it is not – witness the sudden drop experienced by Porsche in the early 1990s. The reason was not as simple as the fact that people suddenly could not afford Porsches – makers of much more expensive saloon cars did not lose sales to the same extent. Buying a car is an emotive decision and many people did not want to be seen driving a sports car at a time of economic crisis. Instead, they spent the same money on a saloon.

Sir William Lyons grasped this before anyone else and resisted any temptation to become too dependent on sports cars. In any case, Jaguar had been so occupied with

The most significant feature on this high-detail cutaway from *The Motor* is the four-wheel disc brakes introduced for the XK150.

its saloon car range that it is almost remarkable that so small a company was able to do as much to the XK150 as it did. After all, 1956 had seen the launch of the new 2.4-litre saloon and also the MkVIII, while the 3.4 saloon was in preparation. New models and new developments came from Jaguar every few months in the second half of the 1950s. It was a time of incredible activity and an air of excitement hung around the marque in a way which is difficult to imagine today – Jaguar had fans.

January 1957, for example, saw the arrival of the XKSS, a road-equipped version of the short-nose D-type with an open cockpit, large windscreen, fixed hood, chromed boot rack and other civilised features. Its engine produced 250bhp (although one has to treat some of Jaguar's power claims with caution because there is a world of difference between what an engine may give on a test rig and when installed in a car), and that meant a top speed of around 150mph with 0-60mph in 5.2sec, which are impressive figures.

The XKSS was a ploy to use up D-type parts. It seems incredible now that people were not queuing round the block for D-types, given the price tag, but this has been rectified by modern makers of 'replicars' which range from plastic-bodied monstrosities to rivet-for-rivet reproductions. Still, 71 D-types were built and that is a fair number for a sports racer of any period. The XKSS

had been in production for just a month when a fire ravaged the factory and the model disappeared from Jaguar's catalogue after only 16 had been made.

If only briefly, the XKSS allowed Jaguar the cachet of marketing the fastest and most exciting production sports car in the world. Later, two owners of D-types would have their competition cars, by then obsolete, converted by the factory to XKSS specification, and some original XKSS models were even converted by their owners into D-types when the historic racing movement – and D-type values – took off. Such cars, however, exist in limbo, being neither fish nor fowl.

Part of the thinking behind the XKSS was that it might compete as a production sports car in SCCA racing, but the only notable competition success it enjoyed was a couple of wins in the Macau Grand Prix, which was then a minor event for amateurs.

When the XK150 was unveiled in May 1957, Jaguar signalled that the car had been aimed at a different sort of customer since it offered only Drophead Coupé and Fixed-Head Coupé models. In fact, most of 1957 production was of the FHC – only 161 DHCs were made in 1957 and just one stayed in Britain. A Roadster did not follow until March 1958, although when it did come on stream it sold more examples in nine months than the FHC or DHC managed in 12. Only two, however, were released to the home market in the first year of production.

The XK150 was the recognisable descendant of the XK120, but the lines had been smoothed and the only

A left-hand drive Roadster, a model introduced in March 1958, nearly a year after the other two body styles. Jaguar's brochure image for the Roadster actually could have been any of the three versions...

THE XK150 JAGUAR ROADSTER

which made the lines appear tail-heavy. As it happens, the overwhelming majority of buyers specified the Special Equipment variant, which were given wire wheels as standard.

Although the radiator grille was broader than on previous models, its many stripes evoked the exquisite grille of the XK120 and it was virtually identical to that of the Jaguar Mark II saloon. The bonnet panel was 4in wider than on previous cars, the gusset used to split the existing panel appearing as a raised line along its length. This improved accessibility to the engine compartment, which improved the temper of many a Jaguar mechanic, but the old XK problem remained of the bonnet occasionally opening at speed. Some owners fitted discreet straps behind the grille to hold down the bonnet. The bonnet panel was always a weak point on the XKs, and Jaguar did not help by offering a 'leaping cat' mascot as an extra. Too often owners used this as a handle, weakening the metal around it, warping the panel and contributing to the inherent problem with the bonnet.

The split, flat-glass windscreen, which should have disappeared years earlier, was replaced by a curved one-piece screen, which greatly improved visibility. A curved rear window on the FHC had the same effect. These features were far from being the 'wrap-round' glassware that was in vogue at the time, but they wrapped round sufficiently to be in the swim of fashion.

There were numerous detail changes: the bumpers were higher and the rear one was in one piece; the rear number plate was on the boot lid in a chromed

panel it had in common with the XK140 was the boot lid. On early models the boot lid was kept open by telescopic struts, but this system was then replaced by a simple stay, as on previous cars, and finally springs were fitted. Apparently, some regular Jaguar customers were caught out by the final arrangement and it was not unknown for them to be struck under the chin by a rising boot lid.

While the lines of the car have often been criticised, to many people's eyes an XK150 with wire wheels is the prettiest car of the family. 'With wire wheels' is an important condition because, as before, pressed steel wheels were standard and cars so fitted also had rear spats,

The Jaguar XKSS in cutaway and in the metal. Created as an expedience to use up D-type components, the XKSS reached a production total of 16 before the factory fire at Jaguar in February 1957.

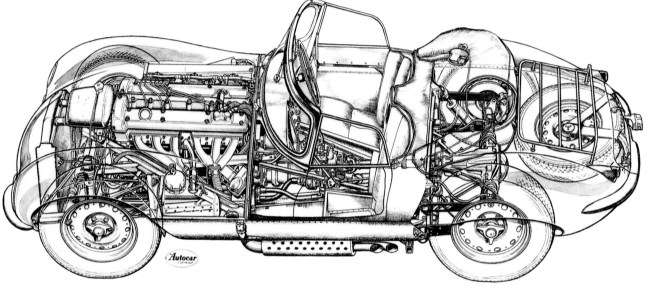

mounting; there were plunger door handles and a 'slide' heater control; the doors were slimmer in section, which added about 4in to the lateral cockpit space; and the inner door panels featured arm rests. The dashboard was redesigned with the two main clocks closer together, and early cars had an aluminium dash which saved a few walnut trees, but before long it was replaced by a padded dashboard covered in leather. Originally the rear lights were similar to those on the XK140, but later cars had a three-lens cluster. If something could be chromed, it was, although not to the point of vulgarity. This is not something you could say of the Corvette, or even of the bodies fitted to some Ferraris.

The chassis remained as on the XK140 – in other words it was still a cut-and-shut MkV and it was at the end of its development. It had been refined and the XK150 had excellent road manners, but they were the road manners appropriate to a high-speed sports tourer. Long gone were the days when Jaguar's XK was the most exciting sports car in the world.

Some types of excitement are not welcome, like not being able to see at night because the lights are inadequate, like not knowing whether the brakes will stop the car, and like wondering whether the traffic will free before the engine boils over. The flaws on the original had all been addressed, and if the XK was no longer the fastest and most stylish sports car in the world, it had grown in competence and, like its predecessors, it was the best bargain on offer.

There were two engine choices at the start. The base unit produced 190bhp at 5000rpm, but few were made and most buyers specified the SE model (with the 'B' cylinder head) with 210bhp at 5500rpm and 216lb ft torque at 3000rpm.

The riverside scene is typically English, but this XK150 Drophead with left-hand drive, body-colour wire wheels and whitewall tyres is destined for America (above). Another Drophead, this time without auxiliary lamps, raises the dust – didn't we see this couple in more love-struck mood on page 61, and with a white car?

There appear to have been different perceptions of the car on each side of the Atlantic, and more American buyers chose the three-speed Borg Warner automatic transmission (with manual overdrive), although this was not to be an option on the S variants. While Americans increasingly saw the XK150 as a grand tourer, the Motor Show guide published by the *Daily Express*, a newspaper not unknown for its xenophobia, called it a 'sporting humdinger' – whatever a humdinger might be.

Even if the XK150 did look as though it was suffering a touch of middle-age spread, it remained incomparable value for money. At around £2000 (including tax and depending on the variant and options) there was nothing to touch it. In 3.4-litre SE trim it could exceed 123mph and cover the 0-60mph dash in 8.5sec, and precious few series-built cars, at any price, could equal that. By the end of the decade a rough pattern would be established: if a

Jaguar cost £2000, then an Aston Martin would cost £4000 and a Ferrari £6000.

Although the Jaguar was unable to match its main rivals, including the Mercedes-Benz 300SL Roadster, in terms of ultimate acceleration, in the hands of most drivers, and on most roads of the time, it could hold its own. More than that, it was more likely to be able to complete a long journey without drama than, say, a Ferrari 250GT or an Aston Martin DB4. The XK150, for all the sniping it has received, was a magnificent car which stood alone in terms of value for money.

It was not value for money, however, which received the headlines – this had become a Jaguar hallmark. It was the fact that the XK150 was a series-built car which offered 12in Dunlop disc brakes on all four wheels. We have already established that the XK150 was not the first car so fitted and, by the time it arrived, Triumph had put

discs on the front of the TR3 as standard, and Jensen offered four-wheel discs as an option on its 541 model. Jaguar, however, had done more to advance the disc brake towards almost universal use than any other maker, and it deserves due recognition. The XK150 may not have been the quickest car in a straight line, but its superior brakes put it into a different class.

Disc brakes were officially an optional extra on the base model and standard on the SE, but nobody has ever seen an XK150 with drum brakes. Even if the styling was beginning to look a little dated, and was no longer at the cutting edge of aerodynamic efficiency, four-wheel disc brakes, together with the world's best mass-produced engine and the cachet of continuing success in international racing, kept the XK150 to the fore in the sports car market.

At the end of 1957 the sports car market looked like this:

	Max speed	0-60 mph	Price (less tax)
AC Ace-Bristol	115mph	7.2sec	£1407
Alfa Romeo 1900SS	112mph	N/A	£2450
Aston Martin DB MkIII	126mph	7.3sec	£2050
Austin-Healey 100-Six	102mph	12.9sec	£762
Chevrolet Corvette★	130mph	5.7sec	£1906
Ferrari 250 GT★★	155mph	8.0sec	N/A
Jaguar XK150	132mph	7.5sec	£1292
Lotus Elite★★★	118mph	11.0sec	£1300
Mercedes-Benz 300SL	130mph	7.6sec	£3100
MGA	98mph	15.6sec	£724
Porsche 1600 Carrera	135mph	10.5sec	£1985
Triumph TR3	103mph	8.8sec	£680

The XK150 in Roadster form, the last model to appear. Body modifications compared with its predecessor are not as substantial as might be expected – the bonnet is an XK140 pressing with an obvious 4in fillet up the centre.

★ Figures for Corvette are for top engine options.

★★ Performance figures for the 250GT varied according to engine option and final drive. A car fitted with a different final drive would have better acceleration and a lower top speed.

★★★ The Elite was announced at the end of 1957, but did not reach full production until 1959. Most cars sold in Britain were supplied as kits to avoid purchase tax.

This list is not comprehensive and is intended to be a rough guide only (and since it reflects the British market, Britons should add 50 per cent to take account of purchase tax). The Aston Martin, Ferrari and Mercedes-Benz were hand-built in small numbers, but it speaks volumes for the XK150 that it naturally calls to be compared with them. Before long the sports car market would be stimulated by the appearance of the Austin-Healey Sprite, which was followed by the MG Midget,

Triple carburettors were among the tweaks for the S version, which took power output to a claimed 250bhp and top speed to 132mph. Badging details describe the model on the nose (below left) and the desirable S specification on the doors (below right).

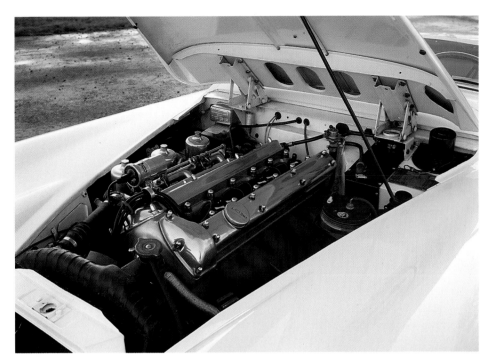

Triumph Spitfire, some specialist British machinery and a succession of small Fiat sports cars.

After a shaky start, the Chevrolet Corvette got into its stride, and while few were seen outside its homeland, it established itself in America. It was cheaper, it could match or even better the XK150 under some road conditions, and its styling was more in touch with its time. On the other hand, it did not have disc brakes, wire wheels were not an option, and it lacked the prestige of wins at Le Mans. In time it would develop into one of the greatest of all lines of sports cars, while Jaguar, which once held the initiative, would stagger in the mire of British Leyland.

The year of the XK150's launch, 1957, was also to be Jaguar's last year of success in international racing until the late 1980s, and Le Mans was the highlight. Five D-types were entered and they finished 1-2-3-4-6. It was perhaps the greatest performance by a marque ever seen at Le Mans, especially when one considers that the opposition was particularly strong that year and, nominally at least, all were private entries. It brought the tally of wins achieved by the 'Wardour Street Bentley' to five, the same as the real Bentley – at the time Ferrari had won Le Mans only twice while Porsche was still disputing class wins.

The winning car, entered by Ecurie Ecosse with

An XK150 Fixed-Head with a Californian licence plate. The proportion of XK exports declined towards the end, but North America always remained Jaguar's largest market.

works backing, had a 3.8-litre engine and Lucas fuel injection. It was a perfect illustration of the way Jaguar's competition programme influenced the road cars: a 3.8 engine would soon become an option for the XK150, while experience with the Lucas fuel injection meant that it would be a long time before a Jaguar production car was fuel-injected.

Mention should also be made of the works Lister-Jaguar which, driven by Archie Scott Brown, dominated British sports car racing in 1957. There had been other Jaguar-engined sports racers built by small companies, most notably by Tojeiro, Cooper and HWM, but none had achieved major success. In each case their appearances in international events were infrequent but even in British racing what successes they had were in minor events.

The Lister was in a different class, being light and controllable, and Lister had a driver of genius in Scott Brown. Archie was born with club feet, short lower legs and a withered right arm which terminated in a vestigial palm and thumb, yet throughout 1957 he often trounced the works Aston Martins and the Ecurie Ecosse D-types.

He started in 14 races, failed to finish in two, was second in one (to Roy Salvadori's works Aston Martin) and won the remaining 11. He created a legend.

Archie's season led to a spate of orders for the Lister, production of the D-type having ended, but in 1958 the WSCC imposed a 3-litre engine limit. Jaguar produced a short-stroke (83mm x 92mm) version of the 3.4-litre engine which gave a respectable 254bhp, but the con-rods were expected to move through impossible angles and frequently broke. Never again would an XK-engined car finish in the top six of a major race. Since then there have been engineers who will say that Jaguar had lost its fine edge of competence, and that there were ways in which the XK engine could have been reduced to a 3 litres without sacrificing reliability or competitiveness.

In any case, the day of the front-engined 'big banger' sports car was fast coming to an end at a serious level. In

Two variations on the XK150 theme. Bertone displayed this elegant coupé at the 1958 Turin Show (left), while this estate car was commissioned by Douglas Hull from an unknown British coachbuilder (below).

club racing, however, D-types continued to be successful on both sides of the Atlantic until around 1960, and in 1958 a secondhand D-type helped to establish the reputation of a young farmer called Jim Clark.

Returning to the road cars, two significant developments arrived in 1958 – the Roadster and the 'S' variants. The launch of the Roadster had been delayed so that the body could be re-engineered, which suggests that Jaguar was taking rather more care over its product than some have suggested. Roadsters were two-seaters and the scuttle was moved back 4in to give a longer, and more aggressive, bonnet and wing line. Since even moving the scuttle back did not absorb all the space of a car which had become, in essence, a 2+2, there was also useful luggage space behind the seats. Padding around the top of the cockpit followed the style of previous Roadsters, but unlike earlier versions the doors were not cut away, and external door handles and winding windows were fitted. Only a masochist would claim that these were not improvements over the old sidescreens, which made the cockpit claustrophobic and restricted the driver's vision.

The S option, which was offered on all variants in February 1959, was a prime example of Jaguar using its careful, if limited, competition programme to improve the breed. At the rear were nine-leaf semi-elliptical springs to firm up the suspension – like all other XKs the springs were encased in leather gaiters. A Thornton Powr-Lok limited slip differential was an optional extra. The engine had a 'straight-port' cylinder head (developed by Harry Weslake), a compression ratio of 9:1, a lighter flywheel and triple SU carburettors. The S produced a claimed 250bhp at 5500rpm and 240lb ft torque at 4500rpm, figures on a par with those of the Mercedes-Benz 300SL and Ferrari 250GT.

Some authorities have suggested that the engine output figures for the S owe more to imagination than to reality, and are for amusement only. The same is also true of most Italian cars of the 1950s. Standard on the S were all the goodies which most of Jaguar's customers were ordering as a matter of course. These included overdrive and wire wheels, which were 60-spoke from June 1958. Top speed increased to 132mph and 0-60mph dropped to 7.5sec.

In October 1959 came further options with the

Tail aspect shows the XK150 Fixed-Head's enlarged rear window, which addressed old criticisms about poor visibility. Beneath the body there was little change from the XK140, with those vestigial rear seats (right) and a similar boot arrangement (below right).

3781cc (87mm × 106mm) engine, a size first used on works D-types. This engine came in two versions: the basic one with the 'B' head gave 220bhp while an S version with the 'straight-port' head produced 265bhp and 240lb ft of torque. This translated into a 0-60mph time of 7.2sec and a top speed of 136mph, which made the XK150 3.8S the world's fastest production car, although a top-spec Corvette was slightly quicker to 60mph.

The 3.8-litre engine hoisted Jaguar higher in the public's perception, although the 3.8S was a rare bird. Only 150 examples of the 3.8S FHC were made, with just 89 DHC versions and a paltry 36 Roadsters. For the discerning observer of the scene, it indicated not so much a serious model option, but rather a sign that something more exciting was on its way – and indeed the E-type was being readied for production. Throughout its

production life, however, the XK150 received almost continuous development and refinement in detail – there was no suggestion that it was a stop-gap.

It appears that a few XK150s were made in 1961, but production essentially ended in late 1960, the last car to be sold in Britain leaving the showroom in November 1960. XKs were in production for 11 years, during which time a total of 31,354 cars were made, and their production level of about 3000 a year was maintained throughout that time.

The XK120 shook the automotive world to its foundations, but by the time the XK150 arrived the extraordinary had become familiar and its image suffered as a result. It was an unfair perception because throughout the XK's life it was at the leading edge of the sports car market even if, after 1951–52, it could not replicate the spectacular competition successes of the early cars.

If excitement was needed, Jaguar had it waiting in the wings. The E-type was unveiled in March 1961 at the Geneva Motor Show, which was the most exciting event in the automotive world since the sheets had first come off the prototype XK120 more than 12 years earlier.

Front and rear views show how far the XK150's appearance had evolved from the original XK120 regardless of the body style.

XKs TODAY

Even under Ford ownership, Jaguar still values its heritage. Chairman Nick Scheele (right) in August 1992 with the XK120 Fixed-Head which broke endurance records at Montlhéry 40 years before, together with drivers Stirling Moss (left) and Jack Fairman (centre).

For today's buyer there is good news and bad news. First the bad news. XKs are not cheap and, as with any car at least 35 years old, every XK either has had the tin-worms exterminated at a cost which is likely to be reflected in the asking price, or else it still has body and chassis rot. There was a time when they were very cheap, however, and many were bought by enthusiasts operating on a tight budget, so stripping away the paintwork can reveal horrors perpetrated by a previous owner who could not afford to have a proper job done.

Although the chassis is simple in concept, it is quite complex in construction, with many overlapping surfaces which are an open invitation to rust. The compound curves of the bodywork are likewise susceptible, since achieving such exquisite shapes in some places required several panels to be welded together, such as in the areas around the headlight pods and the sidelights.

Since the door frames are made of wood, they also rot. There was no way to lubricate the door hinges on the XK120 so they sometimes sag, and nothing spoils a car's appearance more than ill-fitting doors. Many restorers recommend the fitting of steel door frames which, being hidden, detract nothing from a car's visible originality. Another problem is the flimsy XK120 bonnet can be difficult to line up satisfactorily – some original owners fitted leather bonnet straps.

Now for the good news. In the heady days of the late 1980s, when classic cars were seen as blue chip investments, many owners paid a great deal of money to have XKs restored. Following the fall in the market, it has become possible to buy examples for considerably less than the sums paid for their restoration. Since many people over-extended themselves during the classic car boom and were forced to sell, the market has remained fairly fluid and there is perhaps a greater choice of cars for sale than at any time since the 1960s.

For the British buyer there is also the fact that the supply of right-hand drive cars has increased since so many cars returned, particularly from the US, during the boom years. As usual, one should observe that although the description 'California car' is often used in advertisements with the implication that it has been in a benign climate, Northern California can be pretty damp and a car from Malibu can suffer the same ravages from salt as one from Bognor Regis.

Although ground-up restoration can be expensive, the end result is always a beautiful car that should still be capable of 120mph or more, and there is no problem in maintaining one. All body panels are currently available from specialists and there are firms which can refurbish even the delicate radiator grille on the XK120, and others which make the enamel boot badges boasting of Jaguar's wins at Le Mans.

There are firms which offer exchange engines and gearboxes, and engine rebuilds are unusually inexpensive for a car of this performance. Other companies offer exchange instruments and electrical components such as dynamos and starter motors, and these often cost less than a new unit for, say, a Ford Escort. Several trim specialists sell carpets, seat coverings and interior panels, and at least one sources the materials for its kits from Jaguar's original suppliers. Radiators and exhaust systems (in mild steel or stainless steel, and including the twin-pipe 'straight-through' system) are likewise easily obtainable at reasonable prices.

Provided that a car is fundamentally sound and properly protected against corrosion, there is no reason why an XK should not last forever, or even be used as daily transport.

Many owners have uprated their engines, which make them more fun at some fairly insignificant cost to originality. After all, Jaguar continuously improved the engine, which began with 160bhp in 1948 and reached 265bhp with the 3.8-litre S of 1959, so why should the trend not continue? Owners of XK150s can also buy a handling kit (from Harvey Bailey Engineering) which includes Koni or Bilstein shock absorbers, revised spring rates and a stiffer anti-roll bar. This is another upgrade which will not rob a car of exterior originality.

There are strong Jaguar clubs worldwide and generally the magazines they produce are of a high quality. The other services offered will vary, but most clubs are able to offer discounts and advice to members, and there is often a strong social side which can be enjoyable in itself and also a source of tips and information. Not every firm can honestly advertise itself as being the greatest car restorer in the world, for example, and club members will normally be able to steer a new owner in the right direction. Joining a club *before* buying a car of this nature is also a wise move. Before parting with money, you can learn some of the potential pit-falls of purchase, and ownership, from fellow members who love their cars but are not blind to the problems of maintaining ageing machines.

When it comes to choosing the best model of XK, that is a matter of personal taste – they are all wonderful. The original aluminium-bodied XK120 is highly desirable, particularly if it has a competition history. Although none was sold in Britain, 57 right-hand drive cars were made for export to countries such as Australia and South Africa. Other XK120s that are rare with original right-hand drive are the FHC (195 made) and the DHC (294). Any XK120 or XK140 fitted with the full performance pack, which includes a C-type cylinder head, is sought-after.

The rarest of the XK140s is a Roadster with right-hand drive – only 73 were made and just 47 stayed in Britain. Conversions from left-hand drive have increased the stock, but they are still very thin on the ground – and an original right-hand drive car would always be more desirable. Even more rare is the 3.8-litre XK150 Roadster: only 42 were built, while the S version is rarer

RJH 400, an historic rally car from 1954, ran in the Lombard RAC Golden Fifty in 1982. Owner Kevin Donnolly is at the wheel, respected Jaguar writer Philip Porter navigates.

From bare chassis to finished Drophead, XK140s in various stages of build at specialist restorer Vitesse Engineering (left). Autotune (Rishton) Ltd builds an XK Roadster evocation or a dimensionally exact replica of the XK140 Fixed-Head on XJ6 running gear (below).

still because just 36 left the factory. Since there were 888 examples of the 3.4-litre S Roadster, which had performance close to the 3.8-litre S, one of these should be easier on the bank balance.

Since the XK engine remained in production until 1986, it has been used in numerous kit cars and replicas, and not just Jaguars – many other kit cars use running gear from XJ6 saloons. Of Jaguar replicas, most have been versions of the competition cars and they range from evocations of D-types with unconvincing glassfibre bodies to superb reproductions made by concerns like Lynx, Proteus and Wingfield. These usually are not absolutely precise reproductions in every detail, but they are near enough for most people. Absolute perfection costs more than the market would stand. Lynx, however, has built a reproduction of an XKSS which is perfect to the tiniest detail and the owner was delighted to hand over an extraordinary sum for it. Since this occurred after the boom of the late 1980s, it was a case of a wealthy individual knowing precisely what he wanted.

When it comes to the regular XK models, replicas are thinner on the ground. First off the mark was an American firm which marketed the 'Navajo' in 1953. Its glassfibre body followed the XK120 fairly closely, but it was not an exact copy. Its tuned Mercury engine gave it a better 0-60mph time than the XK, but very few were sold. In 1981 an American firm, Coventry Classics, made an accurate replica of the XK120, but it was based on Datsun Z running gear – slightly ironical considering that the Z wiped out the British sports car in America. At

about the same time, a Brazilian company called Fera offered a fibreglass 'XK120' with a locally-built 4.1-litre Chevrolet straight-six engine.

The British company Autotune (Rishton) Ltd makes XK evocations, but because they use the running gear of the XJ6 saloon they have a 7in wider track than the XK120 and cannot be mistaken for one. Although nobody would advance them as an aesthetic improvement, with their more modern mechanicals they can be quicker than the original, and they have better handling and brakes. The same company also makes a more exact glassfibre replica of the XK140 Fixed-Head. In late 1993 a company called Broomstick Cars offered a glassfibre-bodied XK120 kit, based on XJ6 running gear, which received praise from Jaguar authorities for its closeness to the original. One expert, indeed, even suggested that one could buy the glassfibre body to keep an XK120 on the road while its metal body was being restored...

APPENDIX

One of the more unusual optional extras was the pair of fitted suitcases available for the XK120.

Options & accessories ....

Jaguar's options list reflected the dual nature of the XK120. On the one hand you could buy day-to-day items such as a two-piece set of fitted suitcases or a chromed luggage rack, and on the other there were accessories for the sporting motorist. Either way, the options list was not a very long one because the basic car left the factory with a high level of equipment.

Taking creature comforts first, apart from items to improve luggage carrying capacity, one could have one or two Lucas spotlights, a radio (various types of Radiomobile sets), a heater and bucket seats.

For the driver who intended to go racing or rallying, there was the C-type cylinder head, 9:1 compression ratio pistons, a sump guard, aero screen, racing clutch, a cranked gear lever, close-ratio gearbox and a choice of rear axle ratios. There was also an auxiliary petrol tank together with a new spare wheel mounting bracket, since the tank displaced the spare wheel from its usual place in the lower section of the boot.

By the time the XK140 came along, additions to the list were purely cosmetic items such as whitewall tyres and chromed wire wheels, which reflected a changing perception of the car. Competition accessories remained, however, even if they were rarely ordered, and customers who did not have access to good quality fuel could order the 7:1 compression ratio pistons that had been standard issue at the start of the XK120's life.

A Laycock de Normanville overdrive, operating on the top three ratios, was available throughout the XK140's life (and was standard on the 'SE' model), and it was eventually joined by a Borg-Warner three-speed automatic transmission. Extra spotlights and a luggage rack remained options (the fitted suitcases appear to have been dropped) and a new accessory was a windscreen washer.

A radio remained an extra throughout the life of the XK series, but by the time the XK150 appeared the car

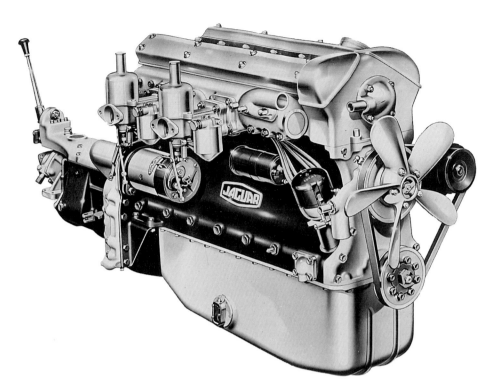

The wonderful XK engine remained in production until 1986, far longer than its designers could ever have imagined. As used in the XK range, its power output grew from 160bhp in the original XK120 to 265bhp in the XK150 3.8S. A company called W.M.Park offered a hard-top for the XK120 Roadster (below) in 1952 – but could this peculiar contrivance really have kept the rain out?

was otherwise so well-equipped that the options list was tiny. Apart from bucket seats, it consisted of minor items such as whitewall tyres, a Jaguar bonnet mascot, anti-glare windscreen glass and a wing mirror. One could still, however, specify a choice of pistons for three different compression ratios.

During the 1950s the accessory business grew strongly and some owners fitted non-Jaguar items such as wood-rimmed steering wheels and 'competition' (in other words, conical) wing mirrors. Opinions today differ about the desirability of such accessories: some people take the view that they detract from a car's originality, but others believe that genuine period features that have been carried for most of a car's life give added character.

Technical specifications....................

Performance figures given are for Roadsters, but they are for amusement only. An FHC could usually reach a slightly higher top speed, but its acceleration was usually slower – except that some magazines sometimes recorded quicker times.

No XK140 was lent to a British magazine for a full road test and the car used by American magazines was a highly tuned 'MC' model with a C-type cylinder head. Since there was always a wide choice of factory-fitted, performance-enhancing engine components and rear axle

ratios, there is no such thing as a reliable set of performance figures for other than individual cars.

The position is further complicated by the fitting of automatic transmission to some later XK140s and many XK150s, although it was not fitted to 'S' models. Owners who did not have access to high-quality fuel could specify a 7:1 compression ratio.

If this was not confusing enough, many authorities query Jaguar's power figures – the horses may have been seen in an engine test shop, but when engines were fitted in cars some of the horses appear to have escaped. There is no accurate record of weights because in the manner of the day they were quoted to the nearest quarter hundredweight (a hundredweight being 112lb or 51kg). Given the range of options, any figures which attempt to be more accurate should be treated with deep suspicion.

XK120

Engine In-line six-cylinder **Construction** Cast iron block, aluminium alloy head **Crankshaft** Seven main bearings **Bore × stroke** 83mm × 106mm (3.27in x 4.17in) **Capacity** 3442cc (210.0cu in) **Valves** Double overhead camshaft, chain driven **Compression ratio** 8.0:1 (7.0:1 or 9.0:1 optional) **Fuel system** Two 1.75in SU H6 carburettors **Maximum power** 160bhp at 5000rpm **Maximum torque** 195lb ft at 2500rpm **Transmission** Four-speed manual **Final drive ratio** 3.64:1 early or 3.54:1 later (4.09:1, 3.77:1 or 3.27:1 optional) **Brakes** Lockheed 12in hydraulic drum brakes with two leading shoes **Front suspension** Independent by torsion bars, double wishbones, anti-roll bar, telescopic dampers **Rear suspension** Live axle, semi-elliptic leaf springs, lever-arm dampers **Steering** Burman recirculating ball **Wheels & tyres** 5J × 16 wheels (5.5J × 16 later), 6.00-16 tyres **Length** 174in (4419mm) **Wheelbase** 102in (2591mm) **Width** 61.5in (1562mm) **Height** Roadster 52.5in (1334mm), FHC & DHC 53.5in (1359mm) **Front track** 51in (1295mm) **Rear track** 50in (1270mm) **Unladen weight** Roadster 26cwt (1321kg), FHC 27cwt (1372kg), DHC 27.5cwt (1397kg) **Top speed** 120mph plus **0-60mph** 10.0sec **Typical fuel consumption** 16-20mpg

XK120 SE (XK120M in USA)

As XK120 except: **Fuel system** Two 2in SU HD8 carburettors with C-type head **Maximum power** 180bhp at 5000rpm (210bhp with C-type head) **Maximum torque** 203lb ft at 4000rpm **Transmission** Four-speed manual with overdrive **0-60mph** 9.5sec

XK140

As XK120 except: **Maximum power** 190bhp at 5500rpm **Maximum torque** 210lb ft at 2500rpm **Transmission** Overdrive and three-speed automatic optional **Rear suspension** Telescopic dampers **Steering** Alford & Alder rack and pinion **Length** 176in (4470mm) **Width** 64.5in (1638mm) **Height** FHC & DHC 55in (1397mm) **Unladen weight** Roadster 27cwt (1372kg), FHC 28cwt (1423kg), DHC 28.5cwt (1448kg) **Top speed** 121mph **0-60mph** 9.2sec

XK140 SE

As XK140 except: **Maximum power** 210bhp at 5750rpm (with C-type head) **Maximum torque** 213lb ft 4000rpm (with C-type head) **0-60mph** 8.4sec (with C-type head)

XK150

As XK140 except: **Final drive ratio** 3.54:1 (4.09:1 with overdrive) **Brakes** Dunlop 12in discs with servo assistance **Length** 177in (4496mm) **Width** 64.5in (1638mm) **Height** FHC 54in (1372mm) **Unladen weight** Roadster 28.5cwt (1448kg), FHC & DHC 28.75cwt (1461kg)

XK150 SE

As XK150 except: **Maximum power** 210bhp at 5500rpm **Maximum torque** 213lb ft at 3000rpm **Top speed** 123mph **0-60mph** 8.5sec

XK150 'S'

As XK150 except: **Compression ratio** 9.0:1 **Fuel system** Three 2in SU HD8 carburettors **Maximum power** 250bhp at 5500rpm **Maximum torque** 240lb ft at 4500rpm **Top speed** 132.4mph **0-60mph** 7.5sec

XK150 3.8

As XK150 except: **Bore × stroke** 87mm × 106mm (3.43in × 4.17in) **Capacity** 3781cc (230.7cu in) **Compression ratio** 9.0:1 **Maximum power** 220bhp at 5500rpm **Maximum torque** 240lb ft at 3000rpm **Top speed** n/a **0-60mph** n/a

XK150 3.8 'S'

As XK150 3.8 except: **Fuel system** Three 2in SU HD8 carburettors **Maximum power** 265bhp at 5500rpm **Maximum torque** 260lb ft at 4000rpm **Top speed** 135.4mph **0-60mph** 7.2sec

Production figures.........................

	Years made	Total
XK120		
Aluminium	1949-50	240
Roadster	1950-54	7374
FHC	1951-54	2680
DHC	1953-54	1767
Total		**12061**
C-type		
Works cars	1951-53	10
Production model	1953	44
Total		**54**
XK140		
Roadster	1954-57	3347
FHC	1954-57	2798
DHC	1954-57	2790
Total		**8935**
D-type & XKSS		
D-type	1954-57	71
XKSS	1957	16
Total		**87**
XK150		
Roadster	1958-60	2264
FHC	1957-60	4448
DHC	1957-60	2673
Total		**9385**
XK150 (production by model)		
FHC	1957-60	3445
DHC	1957-60	1903
Roadster	1958-60	1297
FHC 'S'	1958-60	199
DHC 'S'	1958-60	104
Roadster 'S'	1958-60	888
FHC 3.8	1959-60	656
DHC 3.8	1959-60	586
Roadster 3.8	1959-60	42
FHC 3.8 'S'	1959-60	150
DHC 3.8 'S'	1959-60	79
Roadster 3.8 'S'	1959-60	36
Total		**9385**
Total (all models)		**30381**

ACKNOWLEDGEMENTS

Grateful thanks are due to the owners who allowed their cars to be photographed specially for this book by Tony Baker and John Colley. In chronological order of their cars they are: Michael Stewart (XK120 Roadster & DHC), Michael Fassett (XK140 Roadster & FHC), Hugh Smith (XK150 DHC), Rolf Federer (XK150 Roadster) and Mick Duffy (XK150 FHC). Other cars illustrated in colour were provided by Vic Gill (XK120 Roadster), Peter Sargent (XK120 FHC) and Barrie Williams (XK140 DHC). Mick Duffy, who runs the XK Register of the Jaguar Drivers Club, was especially helpful in locating cars and providing guidance. Peter Richley kindly made available his collection of Jaguar brochures. Archive sources for photographs were *Classic and Sportscar* magazine (thanks to Charlie Pierce and Carol Page), *Classic Cars* magazine (thanks to Nick Kisch, Maurice Rowe and Scilla Robinson), Neill Bruce (who also looks after the Peter Roberts Collection), David Hodges, Philip Porter, Nick Baldwin, Malcolm Bates, Rinsey Mills and Otis Meyer of *Road & Track* magazine. Helpful companies were Vitesse Engineering (01792 310396) and Autotune (Rishton) Ltd (01254 886819).